ROUGH SPIRITS & HIGH SOCIETY

THE CULTURE OF DRINK

ROUGH SPIRITS

SPIRITS

RUTH BALL

& HIGH SOCIETY

BRITISH LIBRARY

THE CULTURE OF DRINK

regonne

emezien

rothm

ur

egnault

wz

ubm

FIRST PUBLISHED IN 2017 BY
THE BRITISH LIBRARY
96 EUSTON ROAD, LONDON NW1 2DB

CATALOGUING IN PUBLICATION DATA
A CATALOGUE RECORD FOR THIS PUBLICATION
IS AVAILABLE FROM THE BRITISH LIBRARY

ISBN 978 0 7123 5215 4

DESIGNED AND TYPESET BY DANIEL STREAT, VISUAL FIELDS
PICTURE RESEARCH BY SALLY NICHOLLS
PRINTED AND BOUND IN THE CZECH REPUBLIC BY P B TISK

FRONTISPIECE │ A bottle of wine takes a glass for a Moselle Galop. │ TITLEPAGE
A barmaid uses early hand pumps to draw a pint of mild. │ TITLEPAGE │ The Duke of
Newcastle, Kit-Cat member and Prime Minister. Engraving after portrait by Godfrey Kneller.
4–5 │ Medieval beer makers at work, from a French Book of Hours, c. 1440–50. │ 6–7 │
Sailors relaxing below decks with a beer among the cannons, 1805. │ 10 │ A merry visit from
the many Spirits of Christmas. │ 11 │ The beautiful friendship between a man and his beer.

CONTENTS

GEORGE IV.

or.

The Spirits of Christmas.

"Black spirits & white,
Blue spirits & grey,
Mingle, mingle, mingle,
You that mingle may!"

Pot Companions — Barclay, Perkins, & Co.

'Come along, my inseparables — when I lose you, I lose the fountain of life. They may call you heavy wet, but there's

INTRODUCTION

There are just three drugs that are generally found to be both legally and culturally acceptable: alcohol, caffeine and tobacco. How acceptable each has been among different social groups and in different cultures has waxed and waned but, since their discovery, none has ever completely gone away. We have fought wars, both military and cultural, to influence the supply of and demand for these mind-altering substances. And they have influenced us in return – both directly and indirectly.

One of their subtlest but deepest influences comes from the creation of new social spaces for indulgence. In Britain, as in other societies, these 'third spaces' – away from the traditional economic centres of the workshop or the marketplace and the social centres of church and home – gave new social and economic forms places in which to grow and flourish. The spaces themselves have also changed and evolved with the birth of these forms, as they left the drinking dens of their birth to take on an independent life of their own, leaving the drinking spaces which had grown to rely upon them to change again or die out.

Alcohol is by far the oldest of the three drugs. The earliest archaeological evidence of its production was discovered in a grave in the Jiahu region of China. The residue of fermented rice, honey, grapes and hawthorn berries found in clay vessels there has been dated to 7000–6600 BC, several thousand years before tea came to dominate the region.

By the Dynastic Period in Egypt, around 3000 BC, there was already a split between the types of alcohol drunk by the upper and lower classes. This same split would be evident in England over 4,000 years later. Workers, right down to the lowliest slaves, drank a daily allowance of beer known as *hqt*, which was heavy with grain and often regarded as a type of food. For food it had a hefty alcohol content, at around 5% ABV, yet the daily allowance for a slave was over ten pints. Thirty units of alcohol daily probably went some way towards keeping the slave population compliant.

The ruling classes, meanwhile, had a taste for imported wine, or *irp*, which came initially from Israel and Palestine but later was also produced in the region. The numerous wines buried with some of the pharaohs give us an insight into how sophisticated the system had already become, with labels distinguishing not only between countries and regions but also individual vineyards producing wines of different characters. Labelling also indicated the quality of the wine, from plain wine – labelled simply *irp* – through good wine – *nfr irp* – to very very good wine – *nfr nfr nfr irp*. But while we know a little about what was drunk by whom and about the ways in which drinking was involved in a handful of religious ceremonies of the era, we know next to nothing about more general drinking habits and cultural attitudes to drinking.

OPPOSITE LEFT | Wine making in Han Dynasty (206 BC–AD 220) China. | OPPOSITE RIGHT A brewing scene from the walls of a tomb at Giza. ABOVE | 'An offering of all things good and pure' at an Egyptian funerary meal including two jars of beer under the table, c. 1295–1070 BC. | BELOW | A post-colonial legend of the discovery of *pulque* by a young girl, Xóchitl, who is presenting it to the King of Tula.

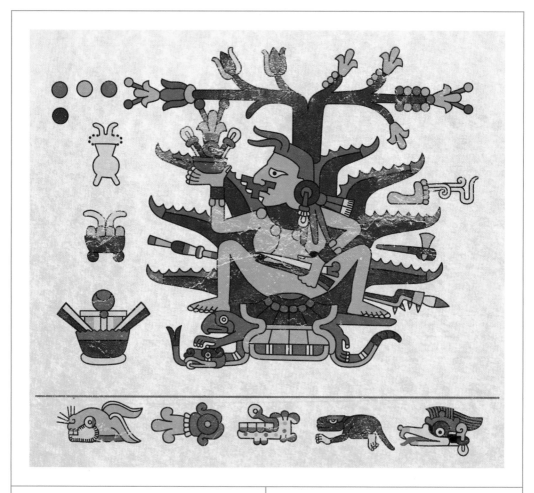

The little more that we know of Aztec drinking culture is even more intriguing. The main drink was *pulque*, and the laws determining who could drink how much, and when, were complex and strictly enforced. Priests, nobility, warriors, brewers and cultivators of the raw maguey used to make the *pulque*, and pregnant women, were all allowed regular draughts of varying amounts. The warriors and brewers were permitted to drink the most, and they took this from troughs filled in honour of the gods in various temples. Those who had made it past the age of fifty-two were allowed to drink whenever they wished in respect for their great age. Only one other group was allowed to drink as freely, as we shall see, but for them it was

their fate and a sign of disrespect.

The gods who ruled over Aztec drinking were the Centzon Totochtin, the 400 divine rabbits, each of which represented a different aspect of drunkenness. To be drunk in Aztec culture was to 'become your rabbit'. They included Tezxatzoncatl, the Straw Mirror, who represented the times you were so drunk that you could see only as well as if looking into a mirror made of straw; Techalotl, who was one of the gods of dance; and Tequechmecauiani, who was the unlikely sounding god of accidentally hanging yourself while drunk – but who may also have represented the death penalty by strangling, which was the punishment for youths who drank in secret outside the permitted days.

The rabbits were the children of the maguey goddess Mayahuel. She had 400 breasts to nurse her 400 children, and she also ruled over one of the periods of the Aztec calendar. Anyone born on the second day of that period, a two-rabbit, was believed to be destined to become a drunk and spend their whole life ruled entirely by the rabbits. As their fate was inescapable they were permitted to drink at any time, and could even use the fact that they had 'become their rabbit' as a defence against any crime. However, although their drinking was inevitable it was not the respected and respectable drinking of the elderly. The two-rabbits were generally disrespected and distrusted, and were not permitted to hold any position of power or authority.

Exemption of the elderly from the normal societal rules governing drinking is a recurrent theme. The writings of the Greeks and Romans provide us with some of the first real commentary on drinking habits outside the ceremonial, although they do write largely about the wine-drinking habits of the upper classes. The most important rule of Greek wine drinking was always to mix it with water before drinking, as the strength of

undiluted wine was believed to make men mad. But when sticking to diluted wine, drinking was generally an accepted, even an essential, part of public life for men. Oration was a key part of that public life, and water drinkers were insulted and considered to be poor orators who would always be cold-hearted by nature and lacking in passion. Women were not supposed to be a part of public life, and by extension were also not supposed to drink, but the literature of the period suggests that many were also dedicated, if secretive, drinkers.

When Plato wrote out his own laws for drinking in an ideal society, he considered that those over forty should drink just as much as they liked, and that others could drink in moderation – but that those under eighteen should not drink at all. Wine was the key to passions and to the truth of the heart, which could be useful in older men, but the young were already too

OPPOSITE | The maguey goddess Mayahuel, depicted with only two of her 400 breasts. | TOP A satyr plays the flute for a maenad, both part of the retinue of the wine god Dionysus. | LEFT | Beautiful youths carrying the tools of the *symposium* decorate this bell krater, a vessel for mixing wine with water, c. 440 BC. | OVERLEAF | Revellers relax, scandalously drinking in the presence of women, c. 480 BC.

excitable. To excite their passions further with wine would be to 'pour fire on fire'. However, as drinking was so important in public life he considered that they should practise drinking to gain strength in it in the same way that they trained in the gymnasium to gain physical strength. The right forum for this training was supposed to be the formal setting of the *symposium*.

The *symposium* took place in a private house for a group of between fourteen and thirty young men. Each began with a meal without wine, and only once that was finished was a *symposiarch* selected to direct the drinking and the entertainment for the evening. This *symposiarch* would determine how much they would all drink and how much it would be diluted; then the group would make a start on the determined quantity and continue until it ran out. These events were supposed to be civilised occasions, with philosophising and other civil pursuits accompanying the drinking, before all the participants finally headed home once they had drunk the full quantity proposed. In practice the drinking clubs formed by young men in Athens, given such sophisticated names as the Autolekythoi (the Wankers) or the Ithyphalloi (the Erections), were so rowdy

OPPOSITE TOP LEFT | Plato teaching at his academy. Roman mosaic from the Villa of T. Siminius Stephanus, Pompeii. | OPPOSITE TOP RIGHT | A nineteenth-century illustration of a Roman dinner party.

OPPOSITE BOTTOM | A nineteenth-century illustration of a Roman dinner party. | ABOVE A nineteenth-century illustration of a Roman taverna.

that one occasion even resulted in war with Megara.

The Romans continued some of the spirit of the elaborate ritual of the *symposium* with their *convivium* dinner parties, but with wine no longer confined only to the time after dinner, and with women more often allowed to take part. These were, however, still the habits only of the rich, and these parties took place in private homes rather than communal spaces. There were taverns, *tabernae*, where the poorer citizens drank, but we know little about the culture of drinking there even though the eruption at Pompeii preserved a generous 118 examples of them in a state of use. Amphorae were preserved in their long serving racks, along with some telling graffiti cursing one of the landlords for his excessive dilution: 'Curses on you, Landlord, you sell water and drink unmixed wine yourself.'

After Rome fell and Europe became more tribal, drinking was for a while less stratified. The parts of Britain that had become Romanised largely lost access to trade for wine, and the Anglo-Saxons who had settled there took mead brewed from honey as their prized and celebratory drink, over the more common ale. Villages centred on the mead hall, where warriors would make mead pledges promising great deeds in battle, drinking in strict order of precedence starting from the hall lord.

The mead hall was usually the home of the local lord and a general centre for the community as well as a drinking space. Entertaining within the home and without a dedicated outside space became the norm for a long period. Even as England slowly grew from fractured tribes into bigger kingdoms, and then a single kingdom, most travellers could still find a welcome in the house of the local lord. The less mobile villagers sold ale to each other in their homes when they had excess to spare, but generally without a single one dominating. Meanwhile the social centre of the village had become the church, which was also a place of drinking at major festivals and significant events in the lives of the villagers. Lowlier travellers unwelcome at the local manor could find welcome at the monasteries, which offered beds, charity and some well-brewed beer to those who needed it.

However, growing numbers of travellers on the roads and the increasing conservatism of the church when it came to drinking and celebration on their grounds would create pressures that led to the slow formation of dedicated entertainment spaces for travellers and locals throughout the thirteenth and fourteenth centuries. By the end of the fifteenth century those spaces had formed into three distinct types: inns, taverns and alehouses.

TOP | A monk sampling perhaps a little too much of the wine under his care. France, thirteenth century. OPPOSITE | A fourteenth-century miniature of the sin of gluttony shows men drinking wine straight from the bottle. | OVERLEAF | An idyllic pastoral painting of May Day outside a small country inn, 1811–12.

CHAPTER ONE

INN

COMMUNICATION

   23

The inn was associated with travel from the very beginning. Until the fifteenth century, travellers on the roads were relatively few, and they could generally depend on the hospitality of the lord of the manor if they were relatively wealthy, of local villagers if they were poorer, or of monasteries and nunneries whatever their status. However, by the end of the medieval period there were greater numbers of travellers on the roads than ever before, and the traditions of hospitality began to break down under the weight of numbers. Accommodations were set up by the church for pilgrims on the main pilgrimage routes, such as the one to Canterbury, in the form of large hostels or bunkhouses, but the large shared rooms and the limited selection of food and drink didn't exactly represent travelling in style.

To meet more discerning, or less austere, tastes secular inns soon began to emerge in the largest towns. London was, as in so many things, a very early starter

and the *Canterbury Tales*, written in the late fourteenth century, begins in the Tabard Inn in Southwark. In that period there was still plenty in the way of alternative accommodation, especially at religious houses, making staying at the inn a definite choice. It is therefore somewhat surprising that among the colourful characters of the inn's paying guests are a monk and a prioress, who certainly could have stayed in a local convent or monastery for free. Their reason for choosing a tavern could of course have been totally innocent: they could simply have wanted to get an early start on their pilgrimage, with the inn better located for the road. However, the text implies that they were straying from the strictures of their faith by staying there, drawn by the free-flowing drink and the chance to mingle with travellers from outside their orders, which also implies that the early taverns were often a little less than reputable.

The dissolution of the monasteries in the 1530s significantly reduced the availability of alternative places for travellers to lodge outside the inns, even as the numbers on the roads continued to increase. Inns began to be found outside the cities and their reputations began to improve, the reputations of their guests improving along with them. Every market town now had at least one inn for the lodging of respectable merchants and other people who had come for the markets. In the same period inland trade, which was the trade between counties, expanded significantly and markets were increasingly

OPPOSITE | A group of pilgrims on the road to Canterbury. From a manuscript of John Lydgate's *Siege of Thebes*, c. 1457–60.

ABOVE/BELOW | A mural of the pilgrims from the *Canterbury Tales*. North Reading Room, Library of Congress, Washington, DC.

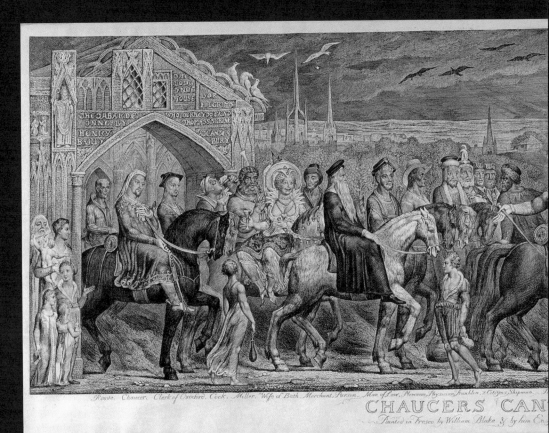

A North East View of the Tuesday Market Place of Lynn Regis

places where wholesalers from across the country came to trade – not just farmers and producers from the local area. The markets themselves were heavily regulated events where major trades such as wool, cloth, grain, malt and agricultural seed were taxed on a local level, with tolls applied by the town authorities. To maintain the authority, and the tax takings, of the market, trading in specific commodities outside the marketplace was often prohibited. The specifics of the regulations varied from town to town, but penalties could be severe. Despite this, the increase in inns that offered storage for goods made the temptation to trade from the comfort of a warm seat by the fire rather than out in a windy marketplace great, whatever the penalties.

Fines and prosecutions for illegal trading away from the marketplace proliferated, but it was clear by the close of Elizabeth I's reign that the authorities were fighting a losing battle. The wholesale trades were moving permanently away from the marketplace and into the inns, and the only real choice was to change the laws and the methods of taxation to accommodate the move. With their development into legitimate trading centres the inns became more than simple lodging and drinking places. Inns were becoming highly respectable, with the innkeeper taking on a position of authority in the community and often growing quite wealthy. However, this newfound respectability did not stop the drink from flowing freely, and the consumption of alcohol was often central to trading. Part of the motivation for the transfer of trade from the marketplace to the inn came from the fact that, traditionally, when larger bargains

PREVIOUS | An etching by William Blake of the pilgrims of the *Canterbury Tales*, 1810. | ABOVE A traditional outdoor marketplace in Lynn Regis growing quiet as trade moves to the inns, 1797. OPPOSITE | An idyllic pastoral painting of May Day outside a small country inn, 1811–12.

had been struck in the marketplace they would be sealed with a drink. The drink was best taken where the other patrons of the inn could act as witnesses to the deal, harking back to the earlier days of the mead pledge. The drinking and trading culture of the inn was born long before the temperance movement could appear and start once more to make drinking incompatible with respectability.

By the sixteenth century most market towns had several inns, and the inns began to specialise in different trades, forming a social hierarchy of a kind. Innkeepers could be promoted if they were doing well, or if the keeper of a better inn left or died to leave a vacancy; if they fell on hard times they might find themselves forced to downsize to a smaller and less prestigious

inn. If a vacancy arose at the very top of the inn hierarchy in a large town there could end up being a general reshuffle, with everyone moving up the chain. In the town of Northampton several such reshuffles were recorded in the ten years from 1736. When a position at the Golden Fleece became vacant the innkeeper of the Sun Inn took the position, and the innkeeper from the Raven, Joseph Williams, took his place. Three years later the Golden Fleece became vacant again and Joseph

OVERLEAF LEFT | The sign of an inn found on the south side of Oxford Street in the late nineteenth century. | OVERLEAF RIGHT | An illustrated card possibly showing that John Shaw could be called upon at the Ram Inn for business, 1790s.

THE SIGN OF THE "MISCHIEF" (*see page* 196).

Williams was able to move further up the chain, although this time he left his own inn to a long-standing servant rather than allow another keeper to move up from the Raven. After another five years the keeper of the very best inn in town, the Red Lion, died. The Red Lion was still just out of Williams's reach – the keeper of the Old Goat Inn took the position – but he was therefore able to take up the vacancy at the Old Goat. By taking his place in the slow upward shuffle he had improved his position three times and attained an inn of some respectability.

The bottom of the hierarchy was occupied by inns such as the Raven, which catered to no trade in particular and were simple, general lodgings and drinking places. Next up would have been the drovers' and carriers' inns on the edges of the towns, which could be fairly profitable but lacked in prestige. They were situated by large pastures and had names that reflected the trade, such as the Fleece, the Lion and Lamb, or the Bull's Head, which were all built on the outskirts of Northampton, where the water meadows provided great pasture. Built more for comfort and practicality than for appearance or elegance, they would have been rambling affairs comprising stables, yards and granaries. Grain was in fact one of the more prestigious commodities to trade, but the deals would already have been arranged at the better inns, using samples – with the carriers who stayed at these rambling inns only transporting the bulk grain that had already been purchased.

Next up the chain came a whole lot of inns specialising in a wide range of trades. While these probably did have an internal hierarchy, the exact nature of it has not been fully recorded. Probably it was a matter of debate even at the time among the minor trades, with the cheese inns believing themselves better than the horse inns, and the horse inns having quite the opposite opinion. As well as cheese inns and equine inns there were cloth inns, where the insides would be white all over

on market day, with undyed samples of cloth laid out for viewing on every surface. There were agricultural seed inns, which were divided again into those specialising in clover or turnip, potato or barley, wheat or grass, with their particular specialities advertised in the local papers. There were hop inns, too, which sold different varieties in bulk to beer producers. The cheese inns had specialities brought in from different regions so that buyers could choose from a wide selection. The leather inns gathered both dealers in freshly tanned leather and cobblers and leatherworkers, who could then buy and sell from the same location. The chosen inns of a particular trade would be advertised in the local papers by groups of traders, and the innkeepers themselves would work hard to attract and retain their preferred trades. They often dabbled in trades themselves or even provided rudimentary banking and financial services to the traders they hosted.

Towards the top of the hierarchy the most important and wealthiest of the trading inns dealt in luxury goods. The most regular trade was in fine, imported cloths – silks, satins and velvet brocades – but the inns dealing in luxuries were generalists. Provided the goods were of high quality anything was welcome to be sold, and so they also hosted a range of more occasional luxury items such as glassware, silverware, books, furniture, carpets, artworks or jewellery, as well as auctions of houses or market gardens. They did not restrict themselves to purely physical commodities either, as they also played host to professionals who

CANVASSING for VOTES. Plate II.

To His Excellency Sr Charles Hanbury Williams Ambassador at the Court of RUSSIA, this Plate is most humbly Inscribd By his most Obedient humble Servant

were offering less tangible services such as travelling surgeons, apothecaries and even occultists. Among these inns was the Red Lion, Northampton's best inn, which had just slipped Joseph Williams's grasp and had also been kept by James Bordrigge, who was from a family of minor Yorkshire gentry.

In the largest towns – the county towns, which were the regional capitals – there might also be two or three county inns. They were at the very top of the hierarchy and had no need to be connected to trade at all. Instead they catered to the growing urban gentry, hosting entertainments and hiring out rooms for functions that demanded catering on a very large scale. Special-occasion feasts and banquets were regularly recorded as hosting one or two hundred people. For particularly momentous occasions the several inns of the town

might even work together, such as for the dinner in Leicester that was thrown to celebrate the hundredth anniversary of William III's landing in England. The dinner was put on by the Revolution Club, and had to be split across three separate inns to allow enough space to host all of the 627 invited guests.

The more regular, annual fixtures might be divided between the inns of the town by gentleman's agreement. The Northampton horse races were a great annual social event and brought the gentry to the town from all over the country. The races were enough of a public event that Lady Jane Compton wrote of her social rival that 'I much wonder Mrs Tate should choose to come to Northampton at so public a time as the horse-races ... I hear a great deal of her in this country not much to her advantage'. The entertainments

extended beyond the race itself, with a dinner and ball on each of the three days of the races. In order to share the spoils fairly the Red Lion, the Peacock and the George took turns hosting a ball each night while the other two inns hosted dining for either the ladies or the men, who dined at separate inns throughout the festivities.

County inns were also the administrative and political centres of the county. During elections candidates would take over a local inn and give out huge quantities of food and drink in a practice called treating, which was a normal (and probably highly enjoyable) part of the political process. Outside the election season they would also act as meeting places for county administrations, and as less formal political clubs. Inns were even used as court rooms for the travelling assize courts and

for the local quarter sessions, which must have involved many a judge presiding over sentencing with a goblet of wine in hand. So much for sober justice.

All these various businesses involved people coming and going, travelling between different inns and different towns, which greatly aided communications around the country. Before the spread of the inn network the only reliable method of sending a letter was to physically send a messenger with it, which was expensive and also left the sender deprived of a member of staff for as long as it took to deliver the letter and return with a reply. The journey could take a fortnight or more each way for longer journeys, not counting the time spent waiting for a reply. For families without staff, or for those who could not spare a staff member for so long, the only way to send a letter was

William Wright.
(Publican, Colonel of
Lumber Troop.)

John Smith.
(Printseller.)

William Hurford.
(Chairman.)

Unknown.   Mr. Clark.

Mark Stevenson.
(Attorney.)

William Hamilton.
(Printer of
Morning Chronicle.)

COURT OF EQUITY. BELL

Published November 1st, 1778, by John Smith,

William Harder.
(Landlord of
The Belle Savage.)

John Russell.
(Broker and
auctioneer.)

George Good.
(Auctioneer.)

Unknown.

John Dighton, sen.
(Printseller and
caricaturist.)

Robert Dighton, jun.
(Painter of picture.)

Mr. Towse.

Thomas Thorpe.
(Proprietor of Globe
Tavern, Fleet Street.)

AGE INN, LUDGATE HILL.

on.   Robert Dighton *pinxit*, Robert Laurie *fecit*.

THE
Carriers Cosmographie.

or

A Briefe Relation,

of

The Innes, Ordinaries, Hosteries

and other lodgings in, and neere London, where
the Carriers, Waggons, Foote-posts and
Higglers, doe usually come, from any parts,
townes, shires and countries, of the Kingdomes
of England, Principality of Wales, as also from
the Kingdomes of Scotland and
Ireland.

With nomination of what daies of

the weeke they doe come to London, and on
what daies they returne, whereby all sorts of
people may finde direction how to receiue,
or send, goods or letters, unto such places
as their occasions may require.

As also,

Where the Ships, Hoighs, Barkes,

Tiltboats, Barges and wherries, do usually attend
to Carry Passengers, and Goods to the coast
Townes of England, Scotland, Ireland, or the
Netherlands; and where the Barges and
Boats are ordinarily to bee had
that goe up the River of
Thames westward
from London.

By *Iohn Taylor*.

London Printed by *A. G.* 1637.

to entrust it to a traveller who was going in the right direction – and hope for the best. These letters were treated with a surprising amount of respect, and most did eventually make it to their destination, but it could take a completely unpredictable length of time, making waiting for a reply a nerve-racking business.

As the inn network developed towards the end of the sixteenth century, you could send your letters with more predictability but also with a complete lack of speed if you entrusted them to one of the common carriers who transported bulky goods between towns. The service was regular but slow, as the carriers' convoys were made up of groups of bulky, heavy goods wagons that would travel only a short distance each day and stop off at an inn to rest every night. By 1637, however, this network had become so regular and predictable that John Taylor published a *Carriers' Cosmography*. This was an early directory consisting of a complete listing of the day and place of departure of just under 200 carriers, travelling from London to almost every part of the country, who might carry letters or packets for a small fee. He compiled it with some difficulty, having to ply the regulars of the inns with significant quantities of ale before they would believe that he was not a government official come to impose a new tax on them.

Taylor himself led an interesting life. Having started out as a ferryman on the Thames, he was appointed in 1605 as the Bottleman at the Tower of London, with the job of rowing out to greet any ship arriving laden with wine and demanding two bottles as the tax due to the Lieutenant of the Tower for safe passage. He became a poet, and was embroiled in a pamphlet war with Thomas Coryat, another big personality whom we will meet later when we look at taverns, after insulting his

writing. As a publicity stunt Taylor once attempted to row down the Thames in a boat made of paper with fish tied to canes as oars, so by comparison navigating a few suspicious carriers should have been easy.

The *Cosmography* is, of course, made up entirely of inns, and some inns repeat several times down the alphabetical listing of towns, indicating that they had become growing transport hubs. Some of their number would soon become a key part of a new service that would eventually make sending letters with the slow carriers seem like a thing of the past: the Royal Mail. However, the Royal Mail did not get off to a fast or efficient start, and for over a century the public could not use it at all. In the early 1500s Henry VIII appointed Brian Tuke to the task of ensuring that royal messages would pass quickly down the Dover Road for communication with the Continent. The system of posts – with fresh horses waiting for messengers along a set route – had been used by the Romans, and there were already a number of post roads established on the Continent, but England lagged behind.

Tuke tried at first to force every town in the kingdom by royal decree to have two fresh horses waiting for the king's use at all times – at their own expense – but the results were not promising. Instead, a number of inns were eventually selected along the desired route and a small basic wage was paid for having horses ready, and later for also providing post boys to carry letters sent along the post road without their own messenger. The wage would not have been enough for an independent operator to survive on, but as innkeepers already had stabling and were staffed at all hours in case of new arrivals it was the perfect sideline, bringing in a little extra money. As a bonus it gave the innkeeper regular access to important news from the capital and the court, as well as local prestige. The innkeepers became the first royal postmasters.

By the end of Elizabeth I's reign there were five post roads. Four went to the ports of Dover, Bristol, Holyhead and Falmouth (via Plymouth). The last post road was the Great North Road, which would later extend from London all the way up the length of the country to Edinburgh. The royal postal system was supposed to take messages only for the Crown and government officials, but postmasters quickly saw that they could augment their meagre salaries by adding a few unofficial letters to the post bag, for a fee. For decades there were occasional half-hearted attempts to put a stop to this. However, the control that London could assert on a system made up not of courtiers, who relied on the court for their power and influence, but of independent local innkeepers, who liked but did not need the extra business, was rather shaky. It became even more difficult to maintain their influence when the salary was slashed in half during Elizabeth I's reign.

It soon became apparent that some ordinary letters were bound to end up travelling with the post no matter how often the postmaster-innkeepers were told not to allow it, because the financial temptation was simply too great and the disincentives too minor. It was eventually officially allowed, even if it was not widely publicised or encouraged. In addition to the Royal Mail and the slow message service of the carriers, there were two rival services operating on the Dover Road, with a series of posts long established by merchants in London for communication with other trading centres in Europe via Dover. These were the Merchant Adventurers, run from London, and the Strangers' Post, operated by Dutch merchants.

Being on the same road, all three services often operated from the same inns along the route, providing triple pay for the lucky innkeepers; such rich rewards would not last. In the tense political times the idea of a foreign post operating unsupervised on English soil made Elizabeth very nervous. Increasing literacy among nobles and merchants made plots arranged by letter more likely than ever, as was proved by the smuggled letters that lost Mary Queen of Scots her head when they were intercepted. The fear of written conspiracy eventually became too great, and in 1591 the Strangers' Post was outlawed and the Merchant Adventurers given a monopoly over posts on the Dover Road, providing they also carried the Royal Mail on that route without charge. The poor innkeepers were reduced from three paymasters to one in a single order. The Dover Road would operate entirely separately from the other post roads for many years, and would generally operate much better as it was kept under the control of the merchants, who were motivated to keep it operating efficiently.

The other posts languished under extremely poor management for decades, with the courtiers who ran them squeezing the postmaster-innkeepers for all kinds of backhanders in exchange for keeping them in place, while also failing to pay their salaries. It was testament to the prestige and other perks that must have come with being the only postmaster in town that innkeepers continued to vie for the role, and to pass it down from father

OPPOSITE | A postman ringing his bell as he walks the streets collecting letters and payment, 1827.

GENERAL POSTMAN.

Pub. by R. Ackermann, London.

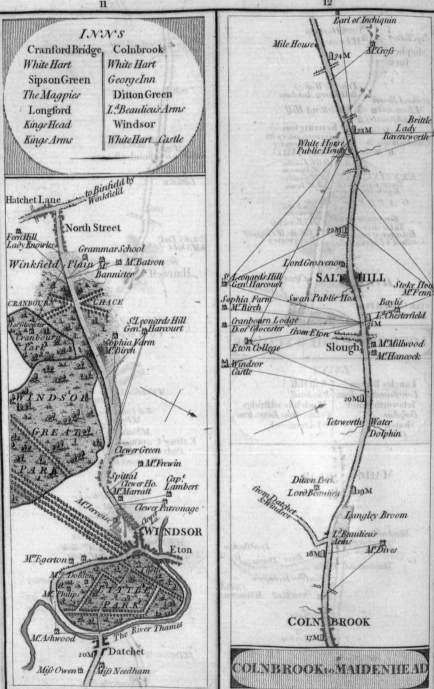

INNS

Cranford Bridge	Colnbrook
White Hart	White Hart
Sipson Green	George Inn
The Magpies	Ditton Green
Longford	Lᵈ Beaulieus Arms
Kings Head	Windsor
Kings Arms	White Hart _ Castle

Hatchet Lane

to Binfield by Winkfield

North Street

Fern Hill
Lady Knowles

Grammar School

Winkfield Plain

Mr Batson
Bannister

CRANBOURN

CHACE

Lᵈ Glocester
Cranbourn Park

Sᵗ Leonards Hill
Gen.ˡ Harcourt

Sophia Farm
Mᵗ Birch

WINDSOR

GREAT

PARK

Clewer Green

Mᵗ Frewin

Spittal
Clewer Ho.
Mᵗ Marratt

Cap.ᵗ Lambert

Mᵗ Jervoise

Clewer Parsonage

Clewr Lo.

WINDSOR

Eton

Mᵗ Egerton

Mᵗ Dolton

Castle

Mᵗ Philips

LITTLE PARK

Mᵗ Ashwood

The River Thames

20M

Datchet

Miſs Owen

Miſs Needham

Earl of Inchiquin

Mile House

24 M

Mᵗ Cross

Brittle Lady
Ravensworth

23 M

White House
Public House

22 M

Lord Grosvenor

SALT HILL

Stoke Hou.
Mᵗ Fenn

Sᵗ Leonard's Hill
Gen.ˡ Harcourt

Swan Public Hoſe

Baylis
Lᵈ Chesterfield

Sophia Farm
Mᵗ Birch

21M

Cranbourn Lodge
D. of Glocester

from Eton

Mᵗ Millwood

Eton College

Slough

Mᵗ Hancock

Windsor
Castle

20M

Tetsworth Water
Dolphin

Ditton Park
Lord Beaulieu

19 M

from Datchet
& Windsor

Langley Broom

Lᵈ Beaulieus
Arms

18 M

Mᵗ Dives

COLNBROOK

17 M

COLNBROOK to MAIDENHEAD

Published by J. Cary July 1ˢᵗ 1790

to son along with the running of the inn, even when the salary stopped coming and the job was costing them money. Petitions did begin to come in from the postmaster-innkeepers to the Crown, starting in 1618 and in increasing numbers in subsequent years. In 1628 a petition came in describing the postmasters as '99 poore men', some of whom 'lye now in prison, and many of the rest daily threatened to bee arrested by reason of their great debts'. The role of postmaster must have been extremely important to these innkeepers if they risked debtors' prison in order to hold on to the roll. Yet their pleading fell on deaf ears; shortly afterwards, in 1635, the Royal Mail was awarded an absolute monopoly on letter carrying throughout the country.

Even though it was inefficient as a letter

service and infuriating to the innkeepers, the monopoly was important for political control: it meant that all letters could now be read by Crown officials before they reached their destination. After the English Civil War (1642–51) the letter office was retained under the control of Parliament. There was even a special device designed for the office that would allow them to open wax seals and reaffix them without any evidence of tampering. Sadly this masterpiece of the spying art was lost when the General Letter Office burnt down in the Great Fire of London. It could never be re-created, as there had only been one in existence. The inventor had taken its secrets to his grave.

The Royal Mail would struggle for another half-decade with many acrimonious internal struggles and some minor improvements in administration, but the changes at the top made little difference to the postmasters in their inns. They continued to sort and distribute mail while the post boys trudged along bad roads on tired old nags and were frequently robbed. It was not until the late eighteenth century

PREVIOUS LEFT | The post road from Colnbrook to Maidenhead with a list of all the inns along the way, 1784. | PREVIOUS RIGHT | Stagecoach designs. ABOVE | The Worcester to London mail coach in full livery, 1808 | OPPOSITE | The Leeds to London mail coach with inside and outside passengers, 1827

MAIL COACH.   Pub. by R.Ackermann.London.

that a great innovation would come about: it would change the nature of the work and of the network, transforming the inns from information centres to major transport hubs on a whole new scale.

Stagecoaches started to appear in the early eighteenth century, as roads and coach technology improved. Running to regular schedules (although advertisements generally carried the proviso 'God permitting' when listing their two- or three-day schedule), the privately run coaches carried four or six passengers inside, as well as large numbers clinging to the roof and the back. Equipped with four or six horses, they greatly reduced travelling times, even though they still stopped overnight at inns, just as the carriers did. They were still expensive, but they did begin to put travel within the grasp of many more people than before. Servants would use the stagecoaches to travel to new positions, as would the better-off tradesmen travelling for commissions. Coaches were even used institutionally, as one inside traveller from Manchester discovered when she was shocked to find her coach

stopping at a house of correction, where ten convicts bound for transportation were loaded on to the roof of the coach above her.

Although the Royal Mail still had an official monopoly, the public could not resist sending messages with the stagecoaches, even if it was against the law. Compared with the official mail they would cut days off the delivery period, arriving in half the time and running to schedule more often too. Besides, the risk was on the coachmen and not on the customers: they were the ones who faced punishment if caught. The few convictions there were for carrying illegal messages were not a sufficient deterrent. Public demand remained high for a service that was simply so much better than the legal alternatives; and with demand high, so was the potential for profit. The mail needed to catch up. It was a man called John Palmer, a theatre owner from Bath, who was largely responsible for bringing the mail into the coaching age. His relationship with the rest of the Post Office was stormy, in part because of his arrogant personality,

MAIDENHEAD INN
ENTERTAINMENT
MAN AND HORSE

Rowlandson 1807

MISERIES OF

Just as you are going off, with only one other person on your side of the coach, who you
Guard &c. — craning, shoving, buttressing up an overgrown puffing, greazy human Hog of
the box to the basket — By dint of incredible efforts and contrivances, the Carcase is
obstructions in the passage.

Pub.^d Feb.^{ry} 15^d 1807 by R Ackermann N°.101 Strand.

...ELLING.
...rself is the last — seeing the door suddenly opened and the Landlady. coachman
...or grazier breed. the whole machine straining and groaning under its cargo from
...weighed up to the door where it has not to struggle with various

STAGE COACHMEN AT THE GOLDEN FLEECE BRIGHTON.

and there was much internal opposition to overcome, but by the beginning of the nineteenth century the mail coach had entered a golden age. Brightly painted coaches, their destinations proudly printed on their sides and scarlet-uniformed guards sounding their horns from the back, raced far ahead of the stagecoaches by not stopping overnight.

The lack of stops made journeys difficult for the five passengers they could carry along with the mail, and reduced the opportunity for the inns to profit from these passengers. Two ten-minute breaks and a twenty-minute break for dinner were all the time they got off the coach in a full twenty-four hours, and wild rumours spread of passengers ending up with 'coach madness'. Luckily the most important innovation by Palmer, the introduction of a regular timetable, allowed the innkeepers at certain stops at least to have a meal waiting for the coaching parties before they arrived. Meanwhile the timetable allowed less than five minutes at other inns along the route for the horses

to be changed and for the incoming and outgoing mail to be exchanged.

It was a difficult job for the deputy postmasters, as the innkeepers running the postal inns were now called, and exchanges often took place at unsociable hours as the coaches drove through the night. A quick change of horses in the

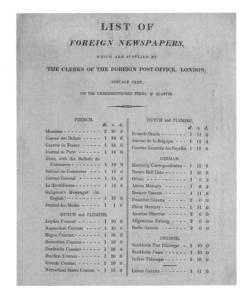

dark at 3am was no easy task. Many coaches now ran so close to timetable that the locals would set their clocks by them, so at least the changeovers were predictable, and it was worth the late nights and the disruption to be the information centre for the town. In a handful of towns the mail would be delivered to the doors of the recipients by foot posts, but most of the time anyone expecting mail would need to come to the inn to collect it. Many people stopped in daily for a drink just to check for mail. An additional perk was that postmasters could be sent newspapers on the mail coaches with no postage fee, which allowed them to fill their rooms with the latest editions for their customers to read ahead of anyone else, as well as to sell copies for profit. All this helped to cement the innkeepers' position as the centre for news and information, connecting the town with the outside world. The guards on the coach would also pass on the freshest gossip to the innkeeper, but this could not always be relied on. For example, when a small group of guards decided to spread false stories as a joke, their tale of fires and riots in London had caused a panic halfway across the country before anyone could get the truth out to quash the rumours. Still, this was a grand time to be a deputy postmaster in a position of power and responsibility in the community.

Meanwhile, at the beginning of the routes in London, getting all the coaches on their way was an operation on an industrial scale. There was room for only nine coaches to collect their mail directly from the General Post Office in Lombard Street, so the others all began their journey at nearby inns. Even the nine

PREVIOUS | A satirical illustration of coach overcrowding, 1807. | OPPOSITE TOP | Coachmen relax at the end of the route at the Golden Fleece in Brighton, 1894. | OPPOSITE BOTTOM | A full list of foreign newspapers that could be ordered by innkeepers from the Foreign Post Office in London. | ABOVE | Multiple mails setting out from the new General Post Office in London.

that started at the office would need to stop at an inn to collect their passengers. There were six main London inns: the Saracen's Head was the starting point for thirty coaches, and the smallest of the six. Three others were all run by the Nelson family – the Bull, the Spread Eagle and the Belle Savage – who were something of a coaching-inn dynasty. The second largest was the Bull and Mouth, which opened a separate booking office in Regent's Circus – the 'Western Coach Office' – and stabled 150 horses for just one of its routes: the Shrewsbury Wonder.

The largest inn was the Swan with Two Necks, which would attract crowds of sightseers every day to watch the full sixty-four coaches depart. They all left simultaneously in a well-organised chore-ography that emerged from the seeming chaos of an inn with 2,000 staff and almost as many horses. The inn was so large and space so valuable that the horses had to be stabled underground. The owner, William

Chaplin, was strict with his staff but had a sense of humour. When he suspected one of his drivers of stealing from the oat bins in the night he hid inside one of them, leaping out on the unsuspecting thief when he opened the lid. It went beyond a joke, though, when he fired the man on the spot.

The days of the brightly painted flying coaches, sounding their horns to warn other carriages to get out of the way, came to an abrupt end just as they seemed at the height of their powers. There was no stopping the unexpected emergence of a much faster form of transport, which had no need for horses or for inns. The railways had come, and by the middle of the nineteenth century the role of the inn as communications hub, business centre and general pillar of the community was already at an end.

The coaches gradually died away as the mail and the passengers were trans-ferred on to the faster trains. With greater

mail volumes providing enough revenue
to support a full-time salary, the role of
distributing the mail was also taken away
from the inns and passed to offices that
could be kept under the complete central
control of the Post Office. Coincidentally,
around the same time the traders who had
dealt from other inns began to profession-
alise themselves as well, setting up corn
exchanges and trading halls. All the trades
and industries that had been born by the
fireplace of the inn had grown up and left
– and without their support most of the
network of inns, hubs of the community,
faded away into history.

OPPOSITE | Mails starting out from the cramped
conditions of the old post office in Lombard Street,
1827. | ABOVE | The yard of the Belle Savage, one
of the Nelson family's London terminus inns.
RIGHT | A coachman wielding his whip from his
seat on the box. | OVERLEAF | Illustration from
The Lawes of Drinking by Richard Braithwaite, 1617.

Hellicon

Aristippu

Agarippe

Hippocren

CHAPTER TWO

TAVERN

SOCIETY

53

W: Hogarth inv.

A MIDNIGHT Mo

N *CONVERSATION*

While inns were widely spread across the country, wherever traffic needed to flow, taverns were a very urban phenomenon. They served wine, and were the only places other than inns allowed to sell it to be drunk on the premises. They generally also offered hot food, but no accommodations: these were places where drinking was the main attraction. Wine was the strongest drink available before the advent of spirits, but it was also expensive because it had to be imported. The combination of the strength of the drink and its price gave taverns a reputation as the playgrounds of the idle rich.

Unlike the inn, where drinking was merely one aspect of the hospitality offered to travellers, alcohol was the raison d'être of the tavern, and it was unashamedly drunk not for sustenance but for pleasure. As in ancient Greece the combination of young, rich men and plentiful drink led to the formation of many societies dedicated to the art of drinking. However, in the context of growing literacy levels and cultural sophistication from around the beginning of the seventeenth century, drinkers were also increasingly preoccupied with ensuring that their drinking companions were witty and influential people – people who could strengthen their own position in society by association and improve their image as learned, modern men.

As the home of the court, the greatest seat of influence in the country, London was also the true home of the tavern. Legislation in 1553 formally restricted these dangerous dens of temptation to cities, incorporated towns, port towns and market towns, and it gave the majority of them permission for only two taverns. A handful of towns, including Oxford and Cambridge, were given permission for three or four, Bristol got six and York managed an impressive eight; but London was head and shoulders above the rest with a full forty licensed taverns.

Some of the liveliest were those based around the Inns of Court, which were not inns in the drinking sense, although the name might cause a little confusion. The Inns of Court were – and still are – the professional associations to which barristers must belong in order to practise. The four surviving Inns of Court all date back to before 1569, possibly much further, and as well as accepting those headed for a serious career in the law, they also

WINE COOPERS.

PREVIOUS | A satirical drawing of a 'Modern Midnight Conversation' of tavern goers in full swing. LEFT | Two wine coopers sample their wares before sale. | OPPOSITE TOP | Young dandies sample wine fresh off the boat at the docks. | OPPOSITE BOTTOM A view of the Mitre Tavern.

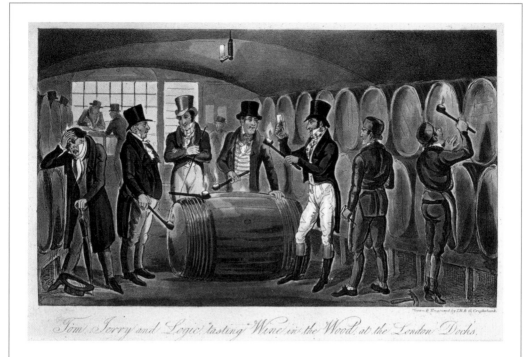

Tom, Jerry and Logic "tasting" Wine in the Wood, at the London Docks.

accepted young aristocrats who required an education in manners, politics and making important friends. They were in many ways 'finishing schools' for rich young men, places where they could study perhaps the most important lesson of all: the art of witty conversation.

The Inns of Court all had their own favoured taverns, and between some there were friendly rivalries, which meant that it was best for them to drink apart. The members of Lincoln's Inn and the Middle Temple remained on friendly terms, though, and their young charges drank together in the Mermaid and the Mitre. Some of their gatherings would go down in history as the meetings of the legendary Mermaid Club.

OVERLEAF LEFT | A tavern, possibly the Mermaid, sits above a lowly alehouse. | OVERLEAF RIGHT An imagined scene: Shakespeare, Walter Raleigh and Ben Jonson drinking with the Mermaid Club. Painting by John Faed, 1851.

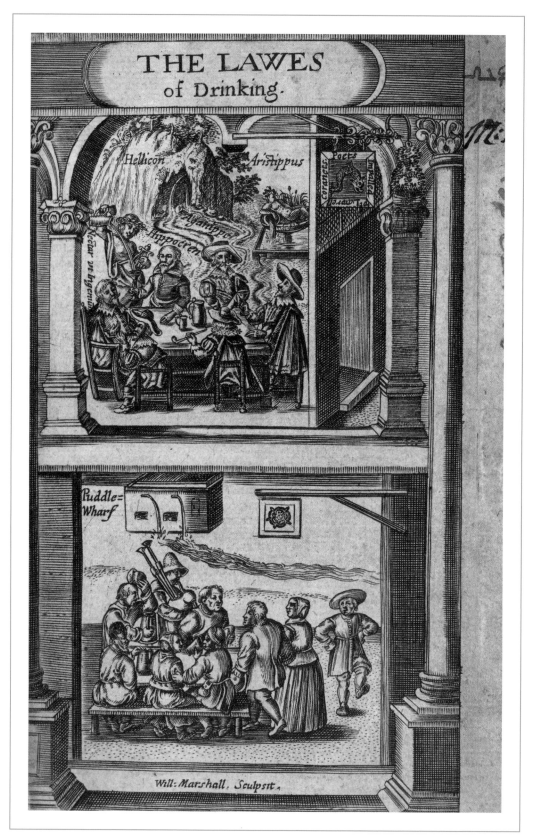

The Mermaid Club, breathlessly written about in the century that followed, was rumoured to have included William Shakespeare, Ben Jonson, Christopher Marlowe, Walter Raleigh, John Donne, John Fletcher, Francis Beaumont and Inigo Jones – along with a whole host of other famous names of their day who are no longer so well known. As with Andy Warhol's Factory, or Woodstock, the legend grew in the years following the meetings until the list included just about anyone who the writers of the lists wished had been there, regardless of evidence or plausibility. It is fun to imagine them all drinking together: Ben Jonson and Shakespeare arguing over whose plays would be remembered the longest, Marlowe passing on his wisdom to the younger men, and Raleigh inspiring all of the writers with tales of his travels.

The legend of their meetings was still inspiring further works as late as 1913, when Alfred Noyes published an entire book of poetry about the imagined happenings at the Mermaid Club, in which he pictured himself transported back to be a pot boy in the tavern, listening in on a meeting. Sadly, for many of these famous names the dates just do not add up. Walter Raleigh was imprisoned in the Tower of London at the time of the supposed meetings, Christopher Marlowe had already been dead for twenty years, and Shakespeare was probably living mostly in Stratford, visiting London only occasionally. Despite a lack of any evidence he was in the club, Shakespeare was acquainted with the landlord of the Mermaid: they purchased some property together in 1613, and he could well have drunk there on occasion and could have bumped into members of the club. He certainly had a

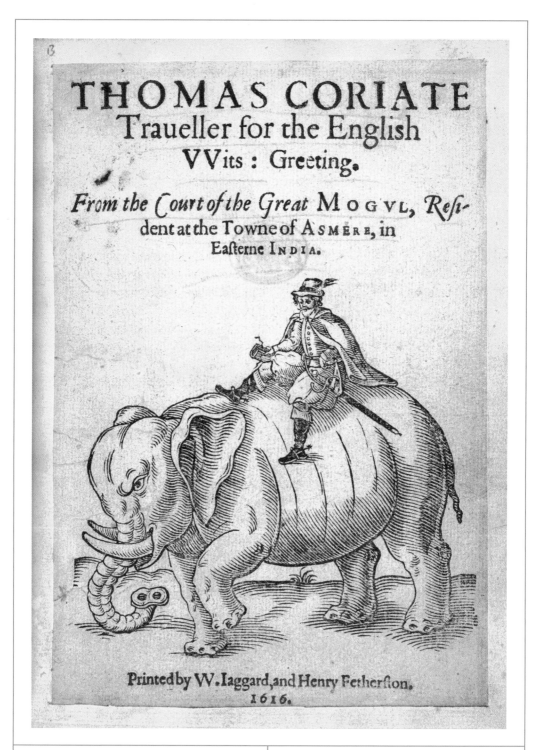

13

THOMAS CORIATE
Traueller for the English
VVits : Greeting.

From the Court of the Great MOGVL, *Resi-*
dent at the Towne of ASMERE, in
Eaſterne INDIA.

Printed by W. Iaggard, and Henry Fetherſton.
1616.

better chance of doing so than Marlowe or Raleigh.

The club also seems unlikely to have been a formal society: it was perhaps more of a joke among friends who often drank together informally but liked to use high, important language among themselves as practice for the formal rhetoric of court. The dramatist Francis Beaumont wrote letters to Ben Jonson in verse while he was living in the countryside. In them he talked of how much he missed the drink and the wit of the company at the Mermaid Tavern: 'words that have been so nimble, so full of subtle flame, as if that every one had meant to put his whole wit in a jest and had resolved to live a fool the rest of his dull life'. The only contemporary record that refers to a formal society rather than a simple meeting of friends is a letter sent from India in 1615 by Thomas Coryat and addressed to 'the High Seneschall of the right Worshipfull Fraternitie of Sirenaical Gentlemen, that meet the first Friday of every Moneth, at the sign of the Mermaid in Bread Street in London'; it included greetings to Ben Jonson, John Donne, Inigo Jones, Robert Cotton and others.

It would be just the style of Thomas Coryat to turn his circle of acquaintances into grand society in his writings. Although he is little remembered, Coryat was a big personality and both popular and well known in his day. He came to fame after writing *Coryat's Crudities*, an account of his journey on foot through France, Germany, Italy and other parts of Europe, which was hugely popular and helped to introduce the English to the fork, which Coryat had encountered in Italy. He was known as a wit at court, where he was popular but also the butt of many jokes: with a reputation for being entertaining but ridiculous, he was something of a court jester.

Coryat's patron, Prince Henry, encouraged the ridicule and even commissioned an entire book of short, mocking verses written by fifty-five of the best-known authors of the day, including many of his drinking friends from the Mermaid. Ben Jonson wrote: 'It is thought he lives more by letting out of air than drawing in; and feared his belly will exhibit a Bill in Chancery against his Mouth for talking away his meals. He is always Tongue-Major of the company, and if ever the perpetual motion be to be hoped for, it is from thence'; John Donne put it thus: 'Therefore mine impotency I confess;/The health which my brain bears, must be far less;/Thy Giant-wit overthrows me, I am gone,/And rather than read all, I would read none'. Meanwhile John Hoskins had his verse comparing Coryat to a porcupine printed with a tune so that readers could sing along, and Henry Peacham wrote his entirely in a made-up language that he called Utopian.

Coryat died only a year after his letter was sent, having walked on foot all the way from Constantinople (now Istanbul) to India searching for material for his second book. He sent back letters, including woodcuts of him riding an elephant and greeting the Great Mogul's pet unicorn. While the friends he left behind may never really have been a 'Worshipfull Fraternitie', the idea of that club inspired later clubs, which were both real and highly influential in shaping Britain as we know it today.

The Hanoverian Kit-Cat Club was one of the most influential of these clubs. It originally met at the Cat and Fiddle Tavern owned by Christopher Cat, who was a pastry cook and famed for his excellent pies. The organiser and founder of the club was a printer, Jacob Tonson, who wanted to bring his authors together with patrons who would fund the printing of

WILLIAM   CAVENDISH

DUKE OF DEVONSHIRE.

JOHN   CHURCHILL

DUKE OF MARLBOROUGH.

JOHN   MONTAGU

DUKE OF MONTAGU.

SIR JOHN   VANBRUGH

RICHARD   BOYLE

EARL OF BURLINGTON.

S.ʳ ROBERT   WALPOLE

SIR RICHARD   STEELE, KN.ᵀ

JOSEPH   ADDISON

ESQ.ʳ

WILLIAM   CONGREVE

ESQ.ʳ

MR JACOB TONSON.

THE FAMOUS SEVEN WONDERS OF THE WORLD

their work. Tonson was an unusual man; in his time printers did not usually curate the work that they printed with anything like the care that he took. Later he was also instrumental in getting copyright laws passed so that authors and, more importantly to him, their publishers would have a chance to fight the cheap, pirated editions of their work that often came out before the official publication.

In shaping the law Tonson was able to ensure that it would also apply to his extensive back catalogue, which give him exclusive printing rights to, among other things, all of Shakespeare's plays. He published them in regular critical editions, which helped to re-popularise the plays a hundred years after the author's death. Tonson also commissioned critical editions of early poetry such as Milton's *Paradise Lost*, arranged a network of translators who would collaborate on larger works, and acted not just as printer but also as editor to Robert Dryden: he was thus more like the first modern publisher than a mere printer.

It was after Dryden's death and from the 'Witty Club' of writers that Dryden had formed in a local coffee shop that Tonson drew the first writers for the Kit-Cat Club. The club originally met in the kitchen of the Cat and Fiddle around the pastry oven, where pies were baked on scraps of discarded paper, and the half-written poetry would be transferred on to the bottoms of the pies. Among the first writers were William Congreve, John Vanbrugh, Matthew Prior and George Stepney. The food and the copious amounts of accompanying wine were paid for by a group wealthy patrons who wished to cultivate the parts of the arts which they thought were being neglected by royal patronage: architecture, music and – most of all – literature, which was hard for the new royal family to appreciate, as they spoke English only as a second language.

However, the patrons also all had something else in common: politics. John Somers had been one of the leading members of the council that invited William and Mary to come and overthrow James II and establish a Protestant, constitutional monarchy. His fellow patrons Charles Sackville, Earl of Dorset, and Charles Montague, Earl of Halifax, had also been involved, and all three became loyal and key members of the new Whig Party, which wanted to keep the power of the monarchy limited as well as ensuring that no Catholic monarch would take the throne.

Acting as patrons of the arts was important to their self-image as men of learning, in the style of ancient Rome, and also as men of wit like the members of the already legendary Mermaid Club and of the later club supposedly formed in the Devil Tavern by Ben Jonson. But having access to young writers eager for their patronage also meant access to potential writers of political propaganda. Drinking with peers of the realm as equals in front of the hot pastry oven of the Cat and Fiddle Tavern must have been as intoxicating as the wine itself – and the writers eagerly agreed to help.

The patronage with which they were rewarded came in the form not only of money but also of salaried government roles, which the peers, as senior members of the government, had it in their power to gift. Some were mere sinecures, by which the holder took the salary and farmed the work out to a lesser-paid secretary, but others were roles of real influence. By the start of the eighteenth century the club had expanded to twenty or thirty strong, with politicians (those with some literary pretentions) being added faster than new authors. Meanwhile the authors were producing regular political pamphlets in support of the Whig Party.

However, the club meetings still revolved around wit and entertainment rather than the politics and power exchanges that held the club together under the surface. First the members would eat a lavish meal of several courses, with peers, dukes and earls calling regularly for more wine to be served to all the diners. It was a more elaborate meal than the few pies

eaten huddled before the oven (although the pies still featured and were enjoyed), and social divisions were back in place to some extent. But the whole company was still treated on a much more equal footing than they would have been outside the club, especially in the case of Tonson, a tradesman, who still took his place as the founder and master of ceremonies.

After the meal the toasting began, providing the main forum for the men of the Kit-Cat Club to demonstrate their wit and good taste. They would propose and vote on various beautiful women to be the subject of the night's toast; and once one was decided on they would compose verses to praise her. The verses were finally engraved with a diamond on a special Kit-Cat toasting glass to commemorate them. The toasting tradition was not exclusive to the Kit-Cats but was also carried on by other societies of the time, including the Knights of the Toast, who dedicated themselves to nothing but drinking and the toasting of beauties.

Robert Walpole, the man who is generally recognised as the first British prime minister (although the role did not yet have that name), had become a member of the Kit-Cat Club by 1703, and he led the Whig MPs in the Commons, who were loyal to the junta of Kit-Cat lords. Not all the MPs were important enough to be admitted to the inner circle of the Kit-Cat Club, and they held their own simpler and more directly political meetings at the Rose Tavern as the Whig Rose Club.

The political power and money with writing and rhetorical talent concentrated in the Kit-Cat Club led, starting with Walpole, to almost every prime minister

PREVIOUS | A rake carouses in a tavern of ill repute, 1735. | OPPOSITE | Ben Jonson holds court at the Devil Tavern.

from 1714 through to 1762 being either a member of or controlled by the Kit-Cat Club. Kit-Cats dominated politics, negotiating the Treaty of Union with the Scottish Parliament, which created the United Kingdom of Great Britain. Kit-Cats even ruled the country as regents for the short period between the death of Anne and the arrival of George I from Hanover. However, they never achieved the lasting effect on the arts that they claimed was their primary aim. The English Baroque style of architecture developed by John Vanbrugh and epitomised by his building of Blenheim Palace was short-lived in popularity. The attempt to encourage the writing and performance of English opera was a complete flop, and few of the literary works by Kit-Cat writers have been remembered as classics.

Their political writings were more widely remembered, especially the periodicals produced in collaboration between Joseph Addison and Richard Steele: the *Tatler*, the *Spectator* and the *Guardian* (the modern papers of the same names are entirely different publications). But most of all the fame of the Kit-Cat Club in its own time created a craze for clubbing in

taverns everywhere, inspired both by rumours about the real club and by Richard Steele's fictional Spectator Club, which featured in every issue of the *Spectator* and was popular and influential nationally.

The Tories set up their own club to rival the Kit-Cat Club, although it never attained the same degree of fame. The Brothers Club met in the Thatched House Tavern, not just on the same day but also at the same time as the Kit-Cat Club, and included among its number Jonathan Swift, author of *Gulliver's Travels*, and Matthew Prior, who had originally been a Kit-Cat but defected to the Tories. They also had their own answer to the Whig Rose Club in the October Club, which formed in 1710 in the Bell Tavern. It was named after the strong October ale that the members liked to drink; and that they were able and willing to drink it in a tavern shows that by this time the divisions between tavern and alehouse were beginning to break down.

Although the distinctions between inns, taverns and alehouses had always been fuzzy around the edges, by the mid-eighteenth century the term 'public house' had started to emerge. This covered both taverns and alehouses, as they

became increasingly hard to distinguish between. The price of wine was falling, making it available to a wider cross-section of society, meaning that taverns were no longer the preserve of the wealthy. Meanwhile the quality of beer had improved, with some of the rich adopting it as a fashionable drink in a way that would have been unthinkable just fifty years earlier.

The Kit-Cat Club never picked up a new membership to replace its leading members as they aged and passed away. By the 1730s the club had ceased to meet – and as a consequence of the changing nature of the drinking places that might have housed them, the clubs of the wealthy and influential that followed on from the Kit-Cat Club were more likely to have their own permanent, private premises.

The Kit-Cats themselves had built a private space for the club out in the countryside at Barn Elms towards the end of its existence, although their town meetings were still held in a tavern, now the more spacious Fountain Tavern on the Strand. Later White's, Boodle's and Brooks's became the main political clubs, and all had their own private premises. This was as a result of the increasing lack of exclusivity in the taverns, and because their members liked to gamble, which was only legal in private clubs.

For the less political the Garrick Club, founded in 1831, featured more of the Kit-Cat Club's stated aim of bringing together artists and wealthy patrons, but it was devoted purely to the theatre. Its private premises offered greater privacy to its members, many of whom have been quite famous, but also for the building of a library of theatrical works. The Athenaeum Club, when it was established in 1830, required all of its members to be 'of distinguished eminence in science, literature or the arts', which is still the membership rule to this day. The establishment of permanent premises gave these clubs a longevity that means they have all survived to this day, albeit going in and out of fashion and with varying levels of influence over the years. They could surely never have enjoyed this longevity by continuing to meet in the back room of a tavern, as much as they owe their origins to those meetings.

OPPOSITE | Thomas Rowlandson, 'The Club Room'. ABOVE | Men talk politics over a punch bowl while the barmaid sees off the advances of one of the customers, c. 1725. | OVERLEAF | A satirical cartoon shows the Whigs overcome with sympathetic tears, 1797.

Tears of Sensibility — Sympathy a Poem — Le...

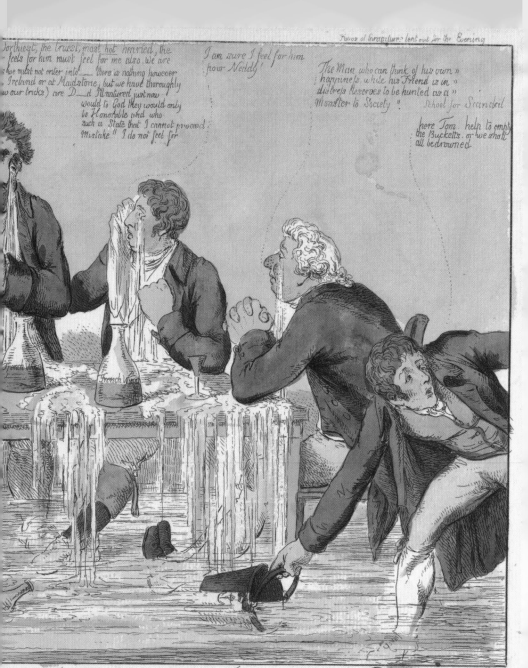

THE
ALEHOUSE
OF THE
PEOPLE

While inns and taverns catered to wealthier customers, alehouses performed the same functions for the poorer members of society. In the Middle Ages, ale selling tended to be informal, with households simply disposing of a temporary excess by selling it to friends and neighbours. If someone in a town or village had some extra ale to sell, they would announce it by putting up an ale stake, a long pole with a bush on the end, outside their home – and when the ale ran out they would take it down again. Ale was also provided to many workers by their employers for free, along with food, during their working day, which meant that there was less need for the workers to buy ale from a specialist drinking place.

Celebrations of the major life events all took place at the church, but were still accompanied by plenty of drink. The church had a much friendlier relationship with drinking during the Middle Ages than it does now. Much of the funding for the local church actually came from the church-ales, which took place on holidays.

The people of the village would contribute grain to a communal brewing for the church-ale, and would then pay to drink for the length of the festival – which could go on for days and involve very heavy drinking indeed. At the church-ale at Deverills in Wiltshire, for example, the tradition was that any bachelors who could still stand on the third day drank for free, but would have to pay if they sat down. Communal drinking sessions could also be held at the church to raise money for local widows or for pilgrims to pay for their journey. It was the thirteenth-century version of a bake sale – but possibly a lot more fun.

The Catholic Church was fairly comfortable in its relationship with communal drinking, but after the Reformation the Church of England became increasingly critical of heavy drinking on church property. Some churches established a separate church house on the edge of the churchyard where traditional communal drinking could take place, apart from the

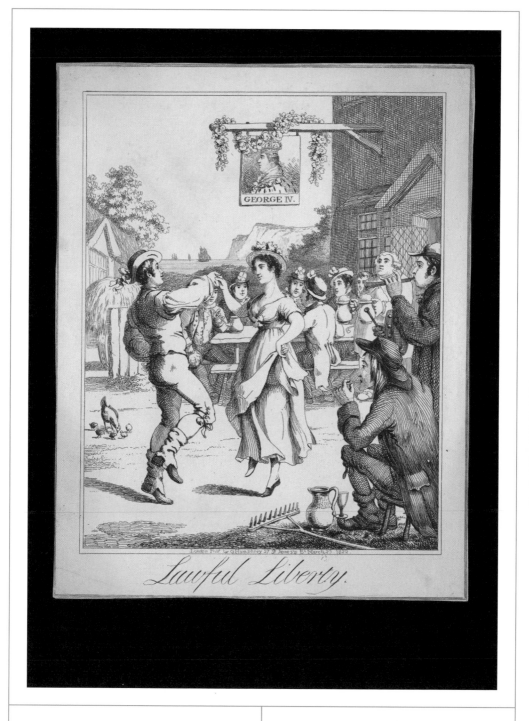

GEORGE IV.

London Pub. by G.Humphrey 27 S. James's St March 25 1822

Lawful Liberty.

PREVIOUS | William Hogarth's 'Beer Street' (detail).
OPPOSITE | A house displaying its ale stake showing ale is available for sale. French, late thirteenth/early fourteenth century. | ABOVE | A young couple dance outside an inn or alehouse, 1822.

OVERLEAF LEFT | The draymen arrive with a delivery of porter and carry it to the alehouse, 1808.
OVERLEAF RIGHT | Alehouse staff see the beer carried down into the cellar, 1827.

THE WEDDING DAY—*all happiness at 'Hawthorne' Hall*—JERRY *and* MARY ROSEBUD *united.*

main place of worship. In other places the drinking parts of the traditional rites of passage were simply transferred to the local alehouse once the church ceremony was complete. Weddings were followed by separate receptions, and baptisms by separate drinking sessions to 'wet the baby's head'.

Permanent alehouses were also made possible by a leap forward in beer

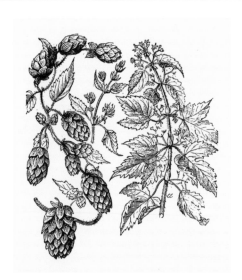

technology: the introduction of hops. Traditional ale made without hops was a thick, muddy drink that spoiled within just a few days and could not be stored for long periods. This was one of the reasons why people had to dispose of their excess to neighbours. The new hopped beer was lighter and tastier, and the resinous compounds in the hops helped to preserve the beer so it could be stored for longer.

Specialist strong beers could even be matured in casks for a year or more, and were often named 'March' or 'October' beers after the best months for producing them. In the spring and the autumn the weather was neither too cold nor too hot, enabling the yeast to produce the strongest beers. As well as being better quality than the old ales, the new beers were cheaper to produce. A total of eighteen gallons of beer could be produced from one bushel of malt, which would only have produced eight gallons of ale.

By the seventeenth century the new beers had replaced the old ales to such an extent that the separate terms were rarely in use, and 'ale' had become a common

BEER STREET.

OPPOSITE TOP | Wedding celebrations continue outside a village alehouse after the church ceremony has finished. | OPPOSITE BOTTOM | A nineteenth-century botanical engraving of hops.

ABOVE | William Hogarth's 'Beer Street'.
OVERLEAF LEFT | Beer advertisement, 1889.
OVERLEAF RIGHT | Ale advertisement, 1882.

WALTHAM BRO'S. Brewers

STOCKWELL, LONDON S.W.

PURE ENGLISH BEERS

The "HALF-GUINEA" ALE 2/6 per Doz.

"S.N." Stout 3/3 per Doz.

"Two-and-Six" Stout 2/6 per Doz.

In Corked & Screw Stoppered Bottles.

TRADE MARK

LA FORGE

LIST OF PRICES In CASKS	Barrel	Kil	Fir	Pin
	36/	18/	9/	4/6
INDIA PALE ALE	54/	27/	13/6	6/9
THE "HALF-GUINEA" ALE	42/	21/	10/6	5/3
AK LIGHT BITTER ALE	36/	18/	9/	4/6
XXXX STRONG ALE (OLD OR MILD)	56/	33/	16/6	8/3
XXX MILD ALE	46/	23/	11/6	5/9
XX MILD ALE	38/	19/	9/6	4/9
X MILD ALE	32/	16/	8/	4/
DOUBLE STOUT	62/	31/	15/6	7/6
S.N. STOUT	50/	25/	12/6	6/3
PORTER	38/	19/	9/6	4/9

TERMS — Cash with Order, or on Delivery, subject to a DISCOUNT on all Beers, except the "Half-Guinea" Ale, of 2s. per Barrel, 1s. per Kil, 6d. per Firkin, 3d. per Pin.

BRANCHES:
Brighton, 144 Western Rd.
Croydon, 107 Parsons' Mead.
Richmond, Grosvenor Buildings.

"No Beer beats Waltham's; the 'Half-Guinea Ale' is by far the best 2/6 Beer on the market." This is everybody's verdict. All Wine Merchants and Licensed Grocers sell Waltham's Bottled Beers. The Beers are bottled at the Brewery. For Cask Beer send direct to the Brewery, or to the nearest Branch as above. Be careful not to address orders to the wrong Brewery; nor allow yourself to be wheedled into buying any other Beer.

Brewery address above—copy this.

IND, COOPE & CO'S

CELEBRATED

ROMFORD ALE.

IN

FINE CONDITION.

—

STRONGLY RECOMMENDED.

IMPERIAL
PINTS,

2/6

PER
DOZEN

IMPERIAL
PINTS,

2/6

PER
DOZEN.

To have Bottled Ale in good condition, the Bottle should be kept upright, retained in that position until the cork is drawn, and the Ale poured carefully into a jug, keeping back the sediment.

D. CLARK,

FAMILY GROCER & BOTTLED BEER MERCHANT,
97, WESTMINSTER ROAD.

ALE BREWER'S DRAYMEN.

Pub. by R.Ackermann, London.

term for hopped beer, with traditional ale rarely drunk at all. However, the new beers were also more time-consuming and technically demanding to produce, leading to a reduction in the home brewing that had traditionally been one of the main tasks in every household. Alehouses sold beer for consumption both on and off the premises, so even beer for drinking at home would increasingly be bought in from the alehouse. Luckily the new-style beer made much more economical use of grain than the traditional ale; this led to a significant reduction in price and made buying it in much more affordable.

When beer was not affordable to labourers and artisans, in periods of unemployment or reduced employment, it could generally be bought on credit – as could basic foods such as buns or cakes, also sold in the alehouse. Eating and drinking on credit at the alehouse was an essential way of getting through a period of hardship for those who were broke but not yet ready to accept the indignity of parish relief. This was often the only credit of any kind available to poorer people. The cheering effects of the alehouse company along with the intoxicating effects of beer on an almost empty stomach would also have helped people through tough times.

By the early seventeenth century some landlords were also providing more formal economic services, lending out money in addition to extending simple credit on their own wares by acting as pawnbrokers. Some of the larger alehouses

TOP LEFT | Ale brewer's draymen, 1827.

TOP RIGHT | A photo of the Oxford Arms taken by the Society for Photographing Relics of Old London in the late nineteenth century.

OPPOSITE TOP | Inside of a Country Alehouse.

OPPOSITE BOTTOM | Trade card for the Collier Brothers brewery in Essex, c. 1890.

in the towns were even issuing their own local currency in the form of lead tokens. In periods of bad and unreliable coinage a token that could be exchanged for beer at a local alehouse may have retained a more certain value than the clipped and often counterfeit coins which were in circulation.

As well as providing economic relief for locals, the alehouse increasingly provided cheap sustenance and lodging for the travelling poor, who were not able to afford the more expensive inns. With some exceptions in the towns, where there were some larger alehouses with guest-rooms, most alehouses were small and accommodation could take forms as basic as some straw on the floor of the taproom. Sometimes travellers would even share the bed of the landlord, squeezing in with him and his wife. Although alehouses had become a permanent place of business by the seventeenth century they were rarely

purpose built, and most consisted of only two or three rooms: a basic parlour with simple benches and stools, and a tap-room that doubled as a kitchen, with the bedroom of the landlord being the only part of the house that did not double as a public space. The drinking vessels were usually blackjacks: leather tankards water-proofed with boiled black tree sap.

Activity often spilled out into the yard

THESE BEERS ARE BREWED BY WHITBREAD & CO.

BEER IN BOTTLE.

WHITBREAD & Cº

IMPERIAL PINTS, PER DOZEN.

LONDON COOPER AND FAMILY ALE . . **2/6**

LONDON STOUT AND PALE ALE . . **3/0**

EXTRA STOUT **3/6**

IMPERIAL HALF-PINTS.

EXTRA STOUT,

PER **2/3** DOZ.

LABELS:
CHOCOLATE LETTERS
ON ORANGE GROUND.

Sold by all Retail Dealers of
Beer in Bottle.

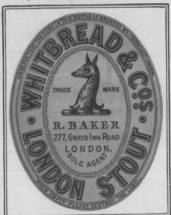

OBSERVE THE CORK IN THIS BOTTLE IS BRANDED WHITBREAD & CO. Lᴰ

WHITBREAD & Cºˢ. Lᵀᴰ.

TRADE MARK

R. BAKER
277, Grays Inn Road
LONDON.
SOLE AGENT

LONDON STOUT

WHEN EMPTY PLEASE DESTROY THE LABEL

IMPERIAL HALF-PINTS.

PALE ALE,

PER **2/-** DOZ.

PLEASE NOTICE
THE TRADE MARK
ON THE CAP.

If any difficulty arises in obtaining
the Beer, the name of the nearest
Retailer will be sent, on application.

MAY ALSO BE HAD IN SCREW-STOPPERED BOTTLES.

BEER IN CASK.

	Pins.	Firkins.	Kilderkins.
LONDON PORTER	—	9/6	19/0
LONDON STOUT	6/3	11/6	23/0
FAMILY ALE	—	9/6	19/0

Discount for Cash on or before Delivery, 3d. Pin ; 6d. Firkin ; 1s. Kilderkin.

BOTTLED BY THEM AT THEIR STORES, 277, GRAY'S INN ROAD, W.C.

Z-one-low....I donna half like
the looks o' tha'

I Put'

Pd.d Aug. 1st 1799 by R. Ackerman Nw Strand.

Etched by Woodward Esqre

A GAME AT PUT IN A COUNTRY ALEHOUSE.

house. This was often the cause of local complaints about the alehouse, when the men relieved themselves in full view of the street.

Up to the early seventeenth century there was little or no control over who could run an alehouse, other than some patchy local regulations. Beer was generally available to alehouses on credit from local brewers, with generous allowances for spoilage and spillage besides, so it was an easy trade to enter. However, sales were also made on credit to customers, and it was easy to get into financial trouble. There were many stories of irate landlords following their customers to their paydays to make sure that theirs was the first bill paid. Landlords who fell deep into debt and could not repay had a bad habit of skipping town and setting up again in the next town, and most landlords stayed in business in one place for less than five years. However, over the course of the next century the drink trade was subject to increasing regulation – the precursors of modern licensing laws – and landlords

found their livelihoods under the control of the judges of the local quarter sessions. By the mid-eighteenth century the alehouse keepers had been transformed into much more professional and respectable members of society, although still with nothing like the social standing of the wealthier innkeepers.

As the profession became more respectable, the economic services offered by alehouse keepers changed. Pawnbroking had become a separate and regulated trade, and landlords who still offered pawn services did so under the table and were more likely to be the minority who had criminal ties and acted as fences, usually in illegal and unlicensed premises themselves. A different financial opportunity arose as workplaces grew larger and progressed towards becoming factories. The large workforce made it increasingly difficult for employers to find sufficient coin to pay all of their workers, especially as reliable small coinage was still in short supply.

The alehouses, which were now also

ELINOVR RVMMIN,

The famous Ale-wife of *England.*

When Skelton *wore the Lawrell Crowne;*
My Ale put all the Ale-wiues downe.

PREVIOUS LEFT | Whitbread & Co. beers available in bottle and in cask, 1888. | PREVIOUS RIGHT TOP Two men at cards in a country alehouse. | PREVIOUS RIGHT BOTTOM | The taproom of a small alehouse

OPPOSITE | Men sit on the traditional bench that was always found at the front of an alehouse. ABOVE | An ancient alehouse serves ale in a pair of leather blackjacks.

less inclined to offer credit, were one type of local business with a large and reliable flow of small coinage. They had also generally grown from small, three-room houses into larger premises, frequently purpose built and with some bigger rooms suitable for private gatherings. The alehouse paytable was therefore quickly established as a convenient way for larger employers to pay their workers. The employers would give banknotes covering the entire cost of their wages for the week to the landlord, who would then provide the small coinage to pay the men, knowing that a large proportion of it would be coming straight back over the bar. The alehouses in Stockport even insisted each man purchase a minimum of one drink to cover their services – and it was easy for one drink to become two, then three ... then four.

Those who were even more willing to collaborate with the employers might agree to become their 'truck shop', with some of the workers' pay issued in tokens that could only be spent on food and drink on the premises. Workers later campaigned vigorously against truck shops, and the practice was eventually outlawed.

Among trades that still consisted mostly of smaller workshops, with employers who required workers with particular skills such as tailors, hatters, printers or carpenters, other alehouses performed an important function as a house of call. (The house of call was a kind of labour exchange, where employers could be sure of finding skilled men when they needed them.) Such trades generally operated a formal apprenticeship system: anyone looking to enter the trade would serve under a master for a number of years, where they would be on a very low wage and had often paid to take up the apprenticeship. However, at the end of their apprenticeship they would become journeymen,

who could travel in search of work and have their skills and expertise recognised in most of the places that they went. They could also expect that one day they might be able to become masters in the trade themselves, setting up their own workshop and joining the craft guild, which would give them a position of authority in the town. Many early town councils consisted of the heads of the local guilds.

The journeymen were not full members of the guild and did not have access to the privileges that went with it, but they did form their own craft clubs, borrowing many of the trappings of the guild to which they aspired to belong. They appointed club officers with formal titles, and they had special signs and passwords that allowed members to be recognised as qualified journeymen at other clubs for the same craft throughout the country, and thus find work as 'travelling brothers'. The regular exchange of journeymen between branches enabled a national network for exchanging news and developments within the trade.

Each local club would use a particular alehouse as its home base, which was widely known and was also its house of call. For example, the London Society of Brushmakers met in the Craven Head in Drury Lane. To ensure that the men received work fairly a 'vacant book' would be kept behind the bar: it kept track of who had been waiting for work the longest and was therefore entitled to the first chance at the next work offered.

By the mid-eighteenth century, in addition to functioning as labour exchanges many of the craft clubs also ran 'box clubs', where members would pay a regular subscription and receive financial help in times of sickness or in old age. The clubs could be very formal affairs that held regular meetings, with fines for non-attendance or bad behaviour. The London Society of Brushmakers gave out fines to members who swore, gambled, arrived drunk, talked politics, failed to stand before speaking or would not shut up when instructed by the chairman. It also attempted to limit drinking at the meetings, even as it accepted some drinking as a necessary part of the proceedings, by providing money from the central fund for three pints per man but also prohibiting members from buying any drink of their own until the meeting was over.

Finding officers who could be trusted with the club funds was difficult, so the landlord of the alehouse where the clubs met was often given a portion of the responsibility. The funds would be put into a large, secure box that always remained on the premises and was fastened with three locks. Two of the keys were held by two separate club officials, and the third by the landlord, so the box could only be opened when all three were present. In the less

literate trades the landlord would often also serve as the treasurer of the club, even providing it with loans in times of hardship. It was worth his investing in a club that provided regular custom from skilled and better-paid workers.

Although the craft clubs provided their members with many benefits, unemployment benefit was not one of them. If jobs became scarce locally some of the club would instead go out 'on the tramp' and travel, generally on foot, to the next town. On arrival they would go to the local house of call for the trade, give the password and be able to put their name down in its vacant book to get work there. Only if work was also in short supply in the new town would they receive a form of unemployment benefit, which would be just enough money for food and accommodation for the night at the alehouse, and to cover travel expenses on to the next town

OPPOSITE | A brushmaker at work. | ABOVE | The trade card of the London Society of Brushmakers, 1782.

– where they might have better luck.

Static unemployment benefits were only ever paid in cases of special hardship, and these had to be put to a vote by the full membership of the club. In bad times this tramping system could lead to a conveyor belt of men walking the length of the country in order to continue receiving a small amount to live on. There were reports of men walking the full circuit and returning to their home clubs without finding any work several times in a row. A full circuit for the brushmakers was 1,200 miles, while for the compositors it was 2,800 miles. When only the youngest and fittest of the members were on the tramp the problems would not be too bad, but when severe shortages of work brought older men out on to the roads it could quickly cause significant health problems, as well as distress for the families they had to leave behind. However, the system did allow craft clubs to form a national network, bringing news of pay and conditions in other areas in times when communication systems were otherwise poor, and this flow of information gave the men some bargaining power with their employers.

While the craft clubs would never have thought of themselves as trade unions in the modern sense, they did represent the earliest national organisations of workers, and would often operate a form of 'closed shop' with members prohibited from working for employers who did not meet certain levels of pay and good basic working conditions. When more recognisable trade unions did begin to form in other industries on a local and then national level, they also found their first home in alehouses; but as the unions came more and more into conflict with powerful local figures, the alehouses that hosted them began to fear for their licences, and relations were often tense.

From the beginning of the nineteenth century alehouse keepers were also losing a lot of their independence, such as their ability to make their own decisions about matters such as whether trade unions should be allowed to meet on their premises. This was because, particularly in towns, the premises themselves were increasingly expensive. Magistrates favoured existing premises for licences and they often prevented new houses from opening, giving existing licensed premises more financial value than just the ordinary cost of the building. With alehouses increasingly unaffordable to those who would run them, but still essential as retail outlets for brewers – who had been aggressively increasing their production – the brewers themselves began to step in. They either provided loans to aspiring landlords or bought properties outright and then installed a landlord of their choice in their direct employ.

The rise of these tied houses put landlords at the mercy not just of the local justices for their licence, but also of their brewer for their lease, and made them increasingly hostile to political meetings on the premises. This period also saw a growing loss of differentiation between the inn and the alehouse, as the railways undermined the importance of the coaching network provided by the inns. This reduced the power and social status of the innkeepers significantly, while at the same time alehouses were becoming larger and more comfortable, and thus more likely to attract customers from higher up the social scale than their traditional patrons. The term 'public house' was first applied to alehouses in the early eighteenth century, and by the early nineteenth it was being applied to alehouses, inns and taverns without distinction.

Although the alehouse was already much changed it was the Beer Act of 1830 that really brought an end to the alehouse

as a unique kind of drinking space. In a somewhat surprising act of legislation the Beer Act set aside all previous licensing laws and allowed beer to be sold without a licence, leading to the opening of a huge number of small beer shops. The laws restricting the sale of wine to taverns were also dropped, which allowed wine to be sold in alehouses much as beer had already been sold in a number of taverns, and removed the last real remaining distinction between the traditional classes of drinking place.

When licensing was reintroduced in 1872 there was a single kind of licence – not the three categories used previously – and the modern pub was on its way, a hybrid mixture of inn, tavern, alehouse and beer shop. There were also newcomers to the victualling market, enterprises that had been developing and beginning to compete with it over the years: the cook shops, which provided cheap food that was ready to eat; the lure of spirits, for the committed drinker; and for those who wanted to sit and do business, perhaps catch up on the news by reading the papers, there was the exclusively male retreat of the coffee house.

ABOVE | A view of a Tottenham brewery.

BOTTOM | A barmaid uses early hand pumps to draw a pint of mild.

r longer Bond of Humankind,   Doubt & Mistrust are thrown on Heaven,   Sad Purchace, of a tortur'd Mind,
ut Bane of every virtuous Mind.   And all its Power to Chance is given.   To an imprison'd Body join'd!
What Chaos such Misuse attends!   Sad Purchace, of repentant Tears,
iendship Stoops to prey on Friends;   Of needless Quarrels, endless Fears,
alth, that gives Relish to Delight,   Of Hopes of Moments, Pangs of Years!)   Wm Hogarth, & Publish'd June
wasted with y̌ Wasting Night: & Sold at

CHAPTER FOUR

CAFFEINATED

TRADING

95

The earliest origins of coffee as a drink are obscure, but the first public places dedicated to coffee drinking were the coffee houses of the Ottoman Empire. As the empire expanded, new public buildings were constructed in each conquered city so the Sultan could demonstrate that the empire was a civilising power, much as would happen with the railways in the British Empire, four hundred years later.

The first buildings generally included a marketplace, a merchant's lodge and – last but not least – a grand coffee house built with wide, lamp-lit galleries and sumptuously decorated in the most fashionable style. However, not all coffee houses were these grand constructions built by the Sultan. Most were smaller affairs run by independent businessmen, and many were little more than a small stall with a few benches running along the sides of the street, for customers to rest on while delivery boys ran out with coffee for nearby businesses. In an Islamic empire in which

CAFETIER MAURE.

the consumption of alcohol was prohibited, these coffee shops of differing sizes and social standings fulfilled many of the social functions performed by taverns and alehouses in England as places to meet, socialise and do business.

English merchants visiting the empire were initially mystified by a drink that they found unpalatable and unappealing. That changed when the Levant Company, which had a monopoly on trade with every country on the Mediterranean east of Italy, set up a permanent presence in some of the coastal cities of the Ottoman Empire, starting from the late sixteenth century. Although the Levant Company merchants were largely restricted to 'factories' – areas set aside for foreign merchants that were transformed into miniature European enclaves where European fashions and manners were imposed – they eventually developed a taste for coffee, and the social life of the factories began to revolve around coffee drinking.

It was returning Levant merchants, wanting to keep up the coffee habit after their return home, who provided the earliest demand for coffee houses in London.

In 1651 the merchant Daniel Edwards, who had married into a family of successful merchants, returned from a period in Smyrna to the five-storey townhouse of his father-in-law. He brought with him a personal servant by the name of Pasqua Rosée. The huge townhouse accommodated the business of the merchants on the bottom two floors: kitchens and warehousing were in the basement, and counting house and retail space on the ground floor. Upstairs were the private accommodations of the family, with quarters for servants and apprentices in the garret rooms of the attic.

Daniel Edwards had returned from Smyrna with a habit of drinking coffee two or three times a day, and his servant Pasqua Rosée was particularly skilled at making it. Edwards's friends and other merchants who were recently returned from the Ottoman Empire visited regularly to share a drink of coffee with him. His generosity with the coffee pot eventually gave him a suspiciously large number of friends. So many were visiting every day to drink coffee with him that their comings and goings began to affect the business of the household. He and his father-in-law, Thomas Hodges, resolved to open a coffee house just like the ones that Edwards remembered from the Levant. This would enable them to take advantage of the obvious market for the product while keeping their stairs clear of excess visitors. Not having the time to run the coffee house themselves, and in any case being prevented from entering a retail business by the arcane rules of the London guilds, they provided financial backing for Pasqua

PREVIOUS | Hogarth's Rake loses everything at gambling in White's, after it had transformed itself from a chocolate shop to a private members' club. OPPOSITE TOP | Coffee vendor in traditional Turkish dress. | OPPOSITE BOTTOM | Turkish coffee house, chromolithograph, 1924. | ABOVE | Coffee house in Cairo, 1849.

Rosée to set up a small coffee business of his own.

The first coffee house in London, in fact in the whole of Europe, was a small shed in the churchyard of St Michael's Church in the City of London, marked by a sign showing Pasqua Rosée in traditional dress. While humble, it was in a great commercial location: St Michael's Alley, which ran alongside the church, was one of the few crowded, narrow thoroughfares that ran through to the Royal Exchange. At the busy exchange merchants congregated from all over the city to do business. However, if a visitor stepped aside from the hustle and bustle of the alleyway for a moment to buy coffee in the churchyard, they could stop and drink it in relative peace and quiet under the arched walkways, or walk in the central garden of the beautiful church cloister nearby.

The success of this little coffee stall attracted the attention of the nearby tavern keepers, who reported Pasqua Rosée to the local alderman for running a tippling house without a licence. Luckily common sense must have prevailed and

shown that coffee was a very different drink from wine and beer, because just a few years later, in 1656, the coffee business had moved to a house, the first real coffee house, on the other side of the alley. Rosée was joined in running the business by Christopher Bowman, an ex-apprentice of Thomas Hodges who held the freeman status needed to run a larger business. Rosée left the country shortly after the new coffee house was opened in unrecorded circumstances, but Bowman continued to use his name and his image to market the virtues of the new beverage to the public.

As well as selling coffee to drink on the premises, Bowman was roasting coffee for sale by the packet to individuals and other coffee houses. Included with every packet was a single printed sheet titled 'The Vertue of the Coffee Drink. First publiquely made and sold in England, by Pasqua Rosée' and filled with extraordinary claims about the benefits of coffee drinking for the health and temperament. At the bottom of the sheet was the line 'Made and Sold in St. Michaels Alley in Cornhill, by Pasqua Rosée, at the Signe of his own Head', which remained long after the man himself had left. The sheet would later be copied by other coffee house owners with their own locations added to the bottom, edited to make even more extravagant claims, and eventually used repeatedly in parodies as an immediately recognisable form of writing. The sheet became an eighteenth-century meme to be changed, copied and transformed, while always remaining recognisable.

But beyond the 'vertues' of the new

TOP | The life of the coffee bean from field to cup, c. 1840. | OPPOSITE | The original pamphlet enclosed in packets of coffee sold by Bowman. | OVERLEAF A fight breaks out in a coffee shop at midnight.

The Vertue of the *COFFEE* Drink.

First publiquely made and fold in England, by *Pafqua Rofee.*

THE Grain or Berry called *Coffee*, groweth upon little Trees, only in the *Deferts of Arabia.*

It is brought from thence, and drunk generally throughout all the Grand Seigniors Dominions.

It is a fimple innocent thing, compofed into a Drink, by being dryed in an Oven, and ground to Powder, and boiled up with Spring water, and about half a pint of it to be drunk, fafting an hour before, and not Eating an hour after, and to be taken as hot as poffibly can be endured; the which will never fetch the skin off the mouth, or raife any Blifters, by reafon of that Heat.

The Turks drink at meals and other times, is ufually *Water,* and their Dyet confifts much of *Fruit*, the *Crudities* whereof are very much corrected by this Drink.

T[ ]iality of this Drink is cold and Dry; and though it be a [ ] neither *heats,* nor *inflames* more then *hot Poffet.*

[ ]th the Orifice of the Stomack, and fortifies the heat with- [ ] good to help digeftion. and therefore of great ufe to be [ ] a C'ocka   oo   i the morning.

[ ]ens the *Spirits,* and makes the Heart *Lightfome.*

g   fore Eys, and the better if you hold your Head o-, an   ne Steem that way.

It fuppreffeth Fumes exceedingly, and therefore good againft the *Head-ach,* and will very much ftop any *Defluxion of Rheums,* that diftil from the *Head* upon the *Stomack,* and fo prevent and help *Confumptions,* and the *Cough of the Lungs.*

It is excellent to prevent and cure the *Dropfy, Gout,* and *Scurvy.*

It is known by experience to be better then any other Drying Drink for *People in years,* or *Children* that have any *running humors* upon them, as the *Kings Evil.* &c.

It is very good to prevent *Mif-carryings in Child-bearing Women.*

It is a moft excellent Remedy againft the *Spleen, Hypocondriack Winds,* or the like.

It will prevent *Drowfinefs,* and make one fit for bufines, if one have occafion to *Watch;* and therefore you are not to Drink of it *after Supper,* unlefs you intend to be *watchful,* for it will hinder fleep for 3 or 4 hours.

It is obferved that in *Turkey,* where this is generally drunk, that they are not trobled with the *Stone, Gout, Dropfie,* or *Scurvey,* and that their fkins are exceeding cleer and white.

It is neither Laxative nor *Reftringent.*

Made and Sold in St. *Michaels Alley* in *Cornhill,* by *Pafqua Rofee,* at the Signe of his own Head.

MIDNIGHT. *Tom & Jerry. at*

Pub.d by Sherwoo

INNOCENCE

VIRTUE

Drawn & Engraved by I. R & G. Cruickshank.

Coffee Shop near the Olympic.

Jones Aug.t 31. 1820.

drink, which were mysterious and end-lessly debated in a society that had barely moved beyond the four humours theory of medicine and was still more than a cen-tury away from discovering caffeine, the coffee houses offered a new kind of social space. The coffee house came into being and proliferated during the stormy polit-ical years leading up to the Restoration. During that period it developed a repu-tation as a haunt of republicans, where the affairs of state and the future of the country could be debated by all comers, which was actually still a controversial idea in itself. The idea of the business of court being debated by common people was considered shocking, almost treason-ous, to many of those in power.

Contributing to this idea was a new

Printed for Henry Rodes near Bride lane in Fleetstr

society formed by James Harrington, author of a thinly veiled political mani-festo published in 1656 as the fictional tale 'The Commonwealth of Oceana'. As the political crises of the late 1650s came to a head he formed his Rota Club in the Turk's Head Coffee House, within a stone's throw of Westminster Hall. Its purpose was to debate every evening the constitution that the country should adopt, but strictly by working through Harrington's proposed manifesto and debating the merits of each paragraph, one paragraph per night. This orderly form of debate was a new idea, and to facilitate it the owner of the coffee house had a special piece of furniture made: a huge, oval oak table with passage cut through the centre that would allow him to serve coffee to all of the debaters without interruption throughout the de-bate. Only those who arrived early enough to secure themselves a seat at the table could take part in the debate, and a vote would be taken on the issue discussed at the end of the night by secret ballot.

The Rota had little real influence on the political future of the country. The republic was soon replaced by a return to monarchy, without any heed paid to the verdict of the much-mocked voting box of the coffee house. However, the Rota Club did influence the public imagina-tion about the nature and purpose of the coffee house. The ideal of the coffee shop that would emerge was one where any man could arrive (never any women) and be seated at the first available seat without regard to rank or station. It was a place where he would be able to debate the issue of the day in sober civility with any man he found himself sitting next to. Sobriety was a key property of the coffee shop, because while it was still debated exactly what the effects of this unique new drink were on the mind and body, it had been established with reasonable

certainty that it did not intoxicate in the same way as wine, beer or spirits. This gave the coffee shop some associations with the Puritans, who rejected such intoxication – though not associations that would be too long-lasting.

Outside the dream ideal of the coffee shop, real coffee shops were fast specialising and aiming to attract particular custom. Near St James's Palace the coffee shops cost more and catered to the upper classes. At St James's Coffee House and at White's Chocolate House, located beside St James's Palace, the most influential gentry of the town would generally gather around noon, after they had risen late and taken a stroll in St James's Park to show off the latest fashions. They would stay to gossip until 1pm, when it was time to head across the road and begin the business of the day at court. Afterwards some would return to White's and remain late, gambling. It was a notorious gambling club, and would later become an equally notorious private members' club.

At White's the coffee was six times the normal price of a penny a cup, and at St James's the dress code was strict, helping the shops maintain their exclusivity among the gentry. Other shops specialised simply because their location made them convenient for men of particular

OPPOSITE | Titlepage to a book of jokes, wise sayings and short stories published to assist those in the coffee house who could not rely on their own wit. ABOVE | Titlepage and frontispiece to a book of collected works by James Harrington. | OVERLEAF LEFT | Broadsheet including an expanded version of the 'vertues' and a set of rules for conduct in the coffee house. | OVERLEAF RIGHT TOP | A coffee house in uproar at the appearance of a rabid dog, c. 1809. | OVERLEAF RIGHT BOTTOM | Dancing lesson in a Bath coffee house from *The Expedition of Humphry Clinker*, 1793.

A BRIEF DESCRIPTION OF THE EXCELLENT VERTUES OF THAT Sober and wholesome Drink, CALLED COFFEE,

AND ITS INCOMPARABLE EFFECTS IN PREVENTING or CURING MOST DISEASES INCIDENT TO HUMANE BODIES.

—Florescet Arabica Planta.

When the sweet Poison of the Treacherous Grape,
Had Acted on the world a General Rape;
Drowning our very Reason and our Souls
In such deep Seas of large o'reflowing Bowls,
That New Philosophers Swore they could feel
The Earth to Stagger, as her Sons did Reel:
When Foggy Ale, leavying up mighty Trains
Of muddy Vapours, had besieg'd our Brains;
And Drink, Rebellion, and Religion too,
Made Men so Mad, they knew not what to do;
Then Heaven in Pity, to Effect our Cure,
And stop the Ragings of that Calenture,
First sent amongst us this *All-healing-Berry*,
At once to make us both *Sober* and *Merry*.
Arabian Coffee, a Rich Cordial
To Purse and Person Beneficial,
Which of so many Vertues doth partake,
Its Country's called *Felix* for its sake.
From the Rich Chambers of the Rising Sun,
Where *Arts*, and all good Fashions first begun,
Where Earth with choicest Rarities is blest,
And dying *Phœnix* builds Her wondrous Nest:
COFFEE arrives, that Grave and wholesome Liquor,
That heals the Stomack, makes the Genius quicker,
Relieves the Memory, Revives the Sad,
And chears the Spirits, without making Mad;
For being a Cleansing QUALITY,
By NATURE warm, Attenuating and Dry,
Its constant Use the sullenest Griefs will Rout,
Removes the Dropsie, gives ease to the Gout,
And soon dispatcheth wheresoever it finds
Scorbatick Humours, Hypochondriack winds,
Rheums, Ptisicks, Palsies, Jaundise, Coughs, Catarrhs,
And whatsoe're with Nature leaveth Warrs;
It helps Digestion, want of Appetite,
And quickly sets Consumptive Bodies Right;
A Friendly Entercourse it doth Maintain,
Between the Heart, the Liver, and the Brain,
Natures three chiefest Wheels, whose Jars we know,
Threaten the whole Microcosme with overthrow;
In Spring, when Peccant Humours Encrease most,
And Summer, when the Appetite is lost,
In Autumn, when Raw Fruits Diseases Breed,
And Winter time too cold to Purge or Bleed;
Do but this Rare *ARABIAN* Cordial Use,
And thou may'st all the Doctors Slops Refuse.
Hush then, dull QUACKS, your Mountebanking cease,
COFFEE's a speedier Cure for each Disease;
How great its Vertues are, we hence may think,
The Worlds third Part makes it their common Drink;
The Amourous Gallant, whose hot Reins do fail,
Stung by Conjunction with the Dragons-Tail:
Let him but Tipple here, shall find his Grief
Discharg'd, without the Sweting-Tubs Relief;
Nor have the LADIES Reason to Complain,
As fumbling Doe-littles are apt to Faign;
COFFEE's no Foe to their obliging Trade,
By it Men rather are more Active made;

'Tis stronger Drink, and base adulterate Wine;
Enfeebles Vigour, and makes Nature Pine;
Loaden with which, th' Impotent Sott is Led
Like a Sowc'd Hogshead to a Misses Bed;
But this Rare Settle-Brain prevents those Harms,
Conquers Old Sherry, and brisk Claret Charms.
Sack, I desie thee with an open Throat,
Whilst Trusty COFFEE is my Antedote;
Methinks I hear Poets Repent th'have been,
So long Idolaters to that sparkling Queen;
For well they may perceive 'tis on Her score
APOLLO keeps them all so Cursed Poor;
Let them avoid Her tempting Charms, and then
We hope to see the Wits grow Aldermen;
In Breif, all you who Healths Rich Treasures Prize,
And Court not Ruby Noses, or blear'd Eyes,
But own Sobriety to be your Drift,
And Love at once good Company and Thrift;
To Wine no more make Wit and Coyn a Trophy,
But come each Night and Frollique here in Coffee.

The RULES and ORDERS of the COFFEE-HOUSE.

Enter Sirs freely, But first if you please,
Peruse our Civil-Orders, which are these.

First, Gentry, Tradesmen, all are welcome hither,
And may without Affront sit down Together:
Pre-eminence of Place, none here should Mind,
But take the next fit Seat that he can find:
Nor need any, if Finer Persons come,
Rise up for to assigne to them his Room;
To limit Mens Expence, we think not fair,
But let him forfeit Twelve-pence that shall Swear:
He that shall any Quarrel here begin,
Shall give each Man a Dish t' Atone the Sin;
And so shall He, whose Complements extend
So far to drink in COFFEE to his Friend;
Let Noise of loud Disputes be quite forborn,
No Maudlin Lovers here in Corners Mourn,
But all be Brisk, and Talk, but not too much
On Sacred things, Let none presume to touch,
Nor Profane Scripture, or sawcily wrong
Affairs of State with an Irreverent Tongue:
Let Mirth be Innocent, and each Man see,
That all his Jests without Reflection be;
To keep the House more Quiet, and from Blame,
We Banish hence Cards, Dice, and every Game:
Nor can allow of Wagers, that Exceed
Five shillings, which oft-times much Trouble Breed;
Let all that's lost, or forfeited, be spent
In such Good Liquor as the House doth Vent,
And Customers endeavour to their Powers,
For to observe still seasonable Howers.
Lastly, Let each Man what he calls for Pay,
And so you're welcome to come every Day.

London, Printed for *Paul Greenwood*, and are to be sold at the sign of the *Coffee-Mill* and *Tobacco-Roll* in *Cloath-fair* near *West-Smithfield*, who selleth the best *Arabian* Coffee-Powder and Chocolate, made in Cake or in Roll, after the *Spanish* Fashion, &c. 1674.

T. Rowlandson delin.t

C. Grignion sculp.t

London Publish'd as the Act directs by J. Sibbald Feb.y 1.st 1793.

businesses: the Grecian by the Inns of Court was frequented by lawyers; the Chapter Coffee House was home to both the printers and booksellers of nearby Paternoster Row and the hacks from Grub Street, which was only a little further away; Man's Coffee House near the College of Physicians was popular with doctors, and would attract some scientists away from their own preferred haunts when they needed to find medical men to consult.

The scientists of the Royal Society, when they weren't seeking out doctors, preferred Garraway's near Gresham College. The coffee house was so popular that the officers of the society met there more often than they did in the college. The less formal atmosphere of the coffee shop allowed the members to conduct business with the artisans and craftsmen who provided their scientific instruments and materials, as well as to engage in freer debate with people with a wider range of views than they would have found within the society. While the free lectures, which the college had been founded in order to

ABOVE | Hogarth's Rake loses everything at gambling in White's, after it had transformed itself from a chocolate shop to a private members' club. **OPPOSITE TOP** | A Hogarth cartoon of men plying their trade in Jonathan's Coffee House as Britannia collapses in a corner and the devil peeks in through a window. **OPPOSITE TOP** | An external view of Garraway's Coffee House.

JONATHAN'S COFFEE HOUSE *or* an Analysis of CHANGE ALLEY
With a Group of Characters from the Life - *Inscrib'd to Jacob Henriques.*

provide, were often under-attended, the demonstrations put on in the coffee shop found a ready audience. For example, Robert Hooke explained the principles of magnetic attraction there, while John Beaumont 'shewd his starr stones.'

Other coffee shops became specialised because particular groups of individuals had chosen them as their own and came daily to hold their own miniature courts. At Will's Coffee House Dryden presided over poets and literary men, from his seat by the fire in winter and on the balcony in summer, until his death in 1700. But it was the coffee shops near the Royal Exchange that put the most work into maintaining their particular customer bases.

The central place of the coffee shops in the lives and businesses of the merchants of the exchange was won by them providing not only coffee and a social space in

which to drink it, but also access to key information on matters of trade collected and distributed by the owners. By becoming trade-specific news centres the coffee shops made themselves an important part of the business of the merchants, and made daily attendance near mandatory for successful trading. Many published the information they gathered as a daily newssheet – but awaiting publication cost valuable extra time, so keeping abreast of the market was still best done in person.

Mr Bridge's Coffee House provided – through a contact at the Custom House – the Bills of Entry, which gave a complete listing of all goods imported through the Customs Office that day and thus likely to come on to the market in the Royal Exchange over the next few days. At Garroway's Coffee House in Exchange Alley (which almost shared a name with the doctors' haunt, but was entirely unrelated) the main business was stocks. In 1689 there were only a handful of joint-stock companies, including the Levant Company and, by far the largest, the East India Company. Garroway's kept a list of the current trading prices of all of them, and published these for distribution nationwide as the daily 'currents'. Other houses kept and published the currents for government bonds, foreign currency exchange and other commodities.

Garroway's would eventually lose its status as the primary house for stock trading to its rival, Jonathan's Coffee House. A Huguenot trader, John Castaing, began publishing in 1698 his own sheet of stock prices, exchange rates and bullion prices twice a week out of Jonathan's Coffee House, as 'The Course of Exchange and Other Things'. He was in at the beginning of a fast-growing market. In the early 1690s the Bank of England had been founded to fund growing government debt; this created a market for trading in government bonds. Joint-stock companies had also become more popular, set up to fund everything from new trades overseas to the improvement of water supplies in the city.

The rapidly increasing range of stocks and bonds to be traded attracted not only traditional merchants and investors, but also men who had developed into specialists. Some merely facilitated trades, simplifying the process by knowing who was looking to buy and who to sell, and helping to introduce them and agree on a fair price for a small commission. These were the stockbrokers, and they were relatively well respected. However, others were attracted to the rapid movement of so much money, and began buying and selling on their own behalf, aiming to

PREVIOUS LEFT | End-of-year news round-up in the year of the South Sea Bubble crash. | PREVIOUS RIGHT | A Hogarth cartoon satirising the chaos of the South Sea Bubble crash. | LEFT | Traders on the floor of the new stock exchange. | OPPOSITE | Insurance men study shipping lists hot off the presses at Lloyd's Coffee House.

make a fast profit. They became known as stock-jobbers, and many in wider society were scared of their role in helping the wheels of this already rapid business turn even faster.

With little time to spare before stock prices moved, the language used in Jonathan's rapidly became shortened and specialised, and it would sound almost incomprehensible to outsiders. A contemporary writer gives us a little sample of the hubbub: 'Tickets – Tickets – South Sea Stocks for the Opening – Navy Bills – Bank Stock for the rescounters – Long Annuities – ... Here Tickets for August – Omnium Gatherum for September – Scrip for the third payment – 3 per Cent. consolidated' ... and all that while waiters also called out for those wanting fresh coffee and messengers came in and out shouting the names of message recipients.

The fast-moving wheels did soon come off, as the launch of the South Sea

Company led to what was possibly the first – and certainly one of the most spectacular – stock bubble. In the course of a single year in 1720, stock in the company shot up in price from £100 to £1,000, launching a great national fervour for investing. The rapidly expanding interest lead not only to further trading in the stock of the South Sea Company itself, but also to the launch of many other questionable ventures primarily designed to create stock for trading, rather than to fund real businesses.

These pseudo-businesses included a company launched to make a gun to fire square cannonballs, a company to make a wheel for perpetual motion, a company for extracting silver from lead and, most famous of all, 'a company for carrying out an undertaking of great advantage, but nobody to know what it is'. It says a lot for the coffee-fuelled madness that gripped Exchange Alley that the man who opened his doors one morning at 9am asking for

Lloyd's Monthly Shipping List.

Con	age	Name, Defcrip. Guns, & Refidence of Owner.	Ton	Captain, or Mafter.	Broker or Owner.	Prefent Situation, Where bound, Obfervations, &c.
	93	A ron b. London	144	J. Lees	Loame & co.	In the river for Freight or Charter.
1	74	Abby, b. 6, of London	154	H. Bagwell	L. Williams	From Liverpool for Dantzic, July 18
2	87	Abby, b. Whitehaven	143	W. Ormandy	Ormandy&Co	From Liverpool for Dantzic, July 18
2	97	Afcona, fn. 4, Lynn	250	G. Boothby	W. Bagge&Co	At Oporto, from Lynn, May 5.
1		Abeona, fm. Guernsey	35	Le Coq	Roberts	C. T. at Southampton, Aug. 14.
	95	Abercrombie, London	615	L. Betts	W. Lenox	East India company's fervice
2	01	Aberdeen, Aberdeen	324	A. Gibbon	Gibbon & Son	From Aberdeen to the Baltic, June 27
1	94	Aberdn. Mercht. fl. Sund.	62	W. Brough	Bodgfon	Coafter in the Sunderland trade.
1	00	Aberdeen Packet, fl. Abdn.	124	G. Wilfon	Lon. Ship. Co	From London for Aberdeen, Aug. 24
1	99	Aberdeen fm.	92	Freeman	Freeman & Co	Scotch coafter
1	98	Aberdeen & Leith Packet,	71	A. M'Donald	Cato & Co.	From Leith for Aberdeen, June 16.
1	90	Aberyftwith, fl. Waterford	48	J. Jones	T. Herbert	At Brifol for Aberyftwith, Aug. 14
2	19	Abigail, b. Liverpool	180	J. Bradley	J. Tarleton	At Jamaica from Africa
1		Abigail, fn.	170	S. Hutchins	L. Ladd	In the Portugal trade
2	84	Abigail, fl. London	81	J. Bayley	A. Copland	
	84	Abigail, b. Hull	80	M. Marchoufe	J. Stothard	In the coafting trade
2	98	Abigail, b. Cork	134	B. Lord	Falconberg.	
1	80	Abraham, Briftol	310	B. Hanfon	V. Capelin	In the Norway trade
3	91	Abra. & Mofes, fl. Bofton	112	T. Barclay	Sheath andco	Bofton coafter.
1	95	Acalus, 2, London	167	W. Young	W. Young&co	In the Portugal trade
1	88	Acafto, * 16, Liverpool	267	Carlifle	J. Shaw	On her paffage to Africa, July 22
2	91	Accomplished Quaker	189		J. Farrat, ju	King's Stairs Rotherhithe, late on fale
2	99	Achilles, b. Sunderland	199	Befwick	B. Atkinfon	At Demerara from London
	00	Achilles, 6, Greenock	266	W. Wood	G. Robertfon	At Jamaica from Greenock, June 18
1	64	Achilles, fn Newcaftle	295	T. Nicholfon	J. Bird	At Liverpool from Memel, Aug. 19.
2	D	Acorn, b. Newcaftle	156	R. Allen	W Turner	Coal trade to London
2	00	Acorn, fn. 2, London	276	R. Smith	W. Garbut	At London, bound to the Baltic.
2	99	Acorn, b. 2, S. Shields	93	Swinburn	Blinkinfop	C. T. at Newc. from Shoreham, Aug. 14
1	84	Acorn, Wells	75	L. Mayes	B. Walker	Coaft trade
2	84	Acorn, b. Scarborough	107	T. Wilfon	R. Marflett	At Sunderland from Milton, Aug. 13.
2	91	Acorn, Whitehaven	82	H. Nixou		
1	94	Actæon, 9, Hull	221	R. Barnes	Emmett&Co.	From London for Riga, July 9.
2	95	Actæon, * 4, London	250	Finlay	Barrett &Co.	In the river from Jamaica, July 19
1	99	Active, 12, Briftol	150	Broadfoot	Anderfon&co	From Brifol for Africa, April 13.
3	88	Active, fl. Frafersburg	69	T. Crombie	J. Dalrymple	Scotch coafter
2		Active, Dublin	173	Barker	Barker	From London for Elbing, May 30.
1	86	Active,	300	Brown	J. Harrifon	In the Baltic trade
2		Active, b. 3, Sunderland	112	R. Canny	Canny	Coafter from Sunderland.
2	88	Active, g. Liverpool	101	P. Carr	P. Carr	Irifh trader.
2	87	Active, b. 4, London	153	Chapman	Branford	In the Mediterranean trade.
2		Active, b. 2, Yarmouth	108	T. Coleman	W. J. Hurry	At Shields from Dantzic, Aug. 21
1	97	Active, b. Yarmouth	83	J. Conyers	W.D. Palmer	In the coafting trade
1	85	Active, 10, Lancafter	255	J. Corless	Rawlinfon	At Liverpool from Jamaica, July 19
2	65	Active, 6, Yarmouth	384	E. Darby	W. Hurry	For Peterfburgh June 21
2	95	Active, Chepftow	216	W. Forfter	J. Hodges	At Hull from London, Aug. 10.
2		Active, b. 8, London	169	Clark	Chefmongers	C. T. to Hull, from Dice Key, London.
1	84	Active, fl. Dublin	57	Finlay	R. Knight	Coafter for London, &c.
2	84	Active, fl. Poole	56	J. Williams	T. Burt	Paf. vef. between Portfmouth and Poole
2	90	Active,	232	Harper	Heath & Co.	In the Portugal trade
2	90	Active, b.	107	G. Hayward	R. Miller	At London for Cork, May 17.
1	84	Active, Liverpool	300	Mills	Cafe & Co.	At Liverpool from Jamaica, July 20
2	95	Active, b. Cork	130	Henderfon	Gutteridge	Trader Ireland to London
1	98	Active, 8, Liverpool	197	J. Hornby	Troughton	At Demerara from Liverpool
2	96	Active, b. Beaumaris	86	W. Griffiths	J. Hughes	C. T. to Dublin, &c.
1	93	Active, fl. Peterhead	68	A. Chriftie	J. Skelton	Scotch coafter
3	8	Active, b. Southampton	23	L. Jenkins	J. Poore	Trader to Liverpool &c.
2	89	Active, b. 14, Liverpool	127	R. Wilding	M. Burnie	From Liverpool for Martinico, April
2	80	Active, b. Guernfey	103	R. Jones	C. Weaver	Trader Irifh and Brifol channel
3	91	Active, b. 10, London		Kitchingman	Kitchingman	From Oporto, July 18
2	77	Active, * b. 2, Yarmouth	81	T. Lone	T. Lone	C. T. to London.
2	98	Active, b. Liverpool	150	S. Lee	Simmons	C. T. to Dublin
1	93	Active, b. 5, Sunderland	204	Davidfon	Lawes & Co.	From London for Peterfburg, Aug. 4
1	95	Active, Dublin	151	M'Arthur	Dennifon	W. I. to St. Vincent's.
1	86	Active, fl. Liverpool	71	M'Crea	Banatine	Trader in the Irifh channel
2	8	Active, fl. Liverpool	81	M'Curdie	Banatine	C. T. to Cork.
1	92	Active, fl.	305	M'Dougal	Dacey & Co.	At Philadelphia from London, Apr. 10.
1	86	Active, Whitby	309	Maddifon	Harrifon	At London, for Stockholm.
2	99	Active, b. Sunderland	167	J. Marks	R. Robfon	In the Sunderland coal trade
1	81	Active, fc. Sunderland	45	Mathewfon	J. Branfton	Sunderland coafter.
3	96	Active, 2, London	231	Millet	Waters	In the river, for Martinico, July 8.
1	89	Active, fc. Dundee	110	J. Mills	Mills, fen.	At Dundee, July 15
1	98	Active, Lancafter	192	W. M'Dowell	A. Worswick	

B.

ROYAL-EXCHANGE, LONDON.

REGULATIONS OF LLOYD's COFFEE HOUSE, LONDON.

WE shall be excused for regularly prefacing this Work with some Acount of the Focus of Action in the first Commercial City in the World ;—a Focus the happy Influence of which diverges in every Direction, and renders Great Britain the Emporium of Commerce, and the Mistress of the Seas.—This Work professes to be an emanation from the same general Sources, diffusing over the British Empire complete and satisfactory Information relative to the Causes of its Wealth and Greatness. We hope to prove ourselves worthy of the useful and important Office we have undertaken, by the unremitting Diligence with which we shall pursue our Object, and by gratifying the Expectations of those Persons to whom we have presumed especially to address ourselves.

LLOYD'S COFFEE HOUSE occupies the range of Rooms which extend along the north and part of the western side of the Royal Exchange, London, and is the principal and only place of resort for the Underwriters, Ship Brokers, and Merchants resident in the Metropolis. None but Subscribers are admitted, and the following are the Regulations of the Room, as they were agreed to by the Committee a few years since.

ALL Subscriptions in Lloyd's Coffee Room are personal; and no one is permitted to continue and transact Business in the Rooms, who has not subscribed £15.

The Subscribers may have a Substitute or Clerk admitted into the Rooms on payment of £15.

Each Subscriber has a White Ivory Ticket, with his name inscribed upon it: and if any Subscriber who has not a Substitute, wishes to leave own for a given time, or is unable to attend from indisposition, he is empowered to give an order in writing, by which his representative may enter the House for the purpose of transacting his Business, which order is however to be given up as soon as the Subscriber returns.

The Books of Arrivals and Losses in the outer Rooms, known by the name of *Lloyd's Coffee House*, are regularly posted up, and the Port Letters are likewise daily copied for the FULL and SPEEDY INFORMATION of THE PUBLIC.

Connected with the establishment of Lloyd's Subscription Rooms, are published by separate Committees of the Underwriters two very correct and useful Registers of all the Shipping which have been or are likely to be Insured at this Coffee House. One of these Registers is published at No. 3, Michael's Alley; and the other at No. 4, Castle Court, Birchin Lane; the Subscription for each including the weekly an immediate £2 deposit on £100 shares in this mysterious and entirely unstated enterprise, which he claimed would somehow yield £100 per year, closed his doors at 3pm £2,000 richer ... and was never heard from again.

The bubble collapsed before the end of the same year in which it began, leaving thousands bankrupt, including many famous men and members of the gentry. Even Sir Isaac Newton lost £20,000, and reportedly said of the collapse that 'I can calculate the movement of the stars, but not the madness of men'. Nonetheless, although the business of the stock market was somewhat reformed it was certainly not stopped.

Until 1761 any man could still walk into Jonathan's and, if he could navigate enough of the impenetrable jargon to make a bargain, buy and sell stocks for himself. However, in that year a group of stockbrokers banded together and paid the owner £1,200 a year for private use of the coffee house for three hours a day. They held on to their privacy for a while, until their right to hold private sessions in a public coffee house was denied in a court case brought by a man who had been ejected from a session. As a consequence of that ruling, the stockbrokers had to leave the conviviality of the coffee house and find their own private premises where they could control entry. This led to the building of the Stock Exchange on Threadneedle Street. The Stock Exchange had a wide-open trading floor on the ground floor, but overlooking it on the balcony there was still a coffee room. The impenetrable jargon remained too, at least until the exchange floors became increasingly occupied by computers at the end of the twentieth century.

Although the Stock Exchange retained some of the habits and mannerisms it had gained in its coffee house of origin

it had lost all connection to the name of Jonathan's. Not so with another financial industry born in a coffee house. By far the most recognisable name in the business of information-gathering is that of Edward Lloyd and his Lloyd's Coffee House, which he opened in 1687 in Tower Street, near the Navy Office, but which later moved to Lombard Street to be closer to the Royal Exchange and the Post Office. Through a system of correspondents Lloyd's aimed to be the first place in London to hear of ships arriving safely in any port in Britain. The news as it arrived was read out by the waiters from a special lectern on the first floor and then posted to a noticeboard. It was only to be published in the newssheet, which would later be titled the Lloyd's List, on the following day.

The constant stream of up-to-date information coming from the lectern made Lloyd's the only place to be for insurers of ships, desperate to hear if their latest gambles had paid off when the ships they had insured came safe into port. The bulk of the insurers gathered there, and they were also joined by the underwriters who provided the money that backed them. The insurance trade was loyal to Lloyd's Coffee House for more than a generation until, in 1769, a committee of the trade decided to open their own coffee house across the road. They had become frustrated with the owners' refusal to exclude men they regarded as reckless gamblers. Unlike the stockbrokers, when they moved they decided to take the name with them, naming their establishment the New Lloyd's Coffee House.

PREVIOUS LEFT | Part of the Lloyd's Monthly Shipping List. | PREVIOUS RIGHT | Rules and regulations of the new Lloyd's Coffee House, 1801. OPPOSITE | View of the atrium of the modern Lloyd's Building.

Just four years later they moved the coffee house again to a pair of rooms on the upper floor of the Royal Exchange, where they closed it to the public, requiring an annual subscription for access, restricted to a select group of members. Lloyd's remained there for 150 years until it took its first dedicated building in the 1920s. It is now housed in the Lloyd's Building in London, which is the youngest Grade I listed building in the country. It is a striking modern structure of glass and steel built in 1986, with one entrance that retains just the façade of the older brick building that preceded it. The modern building is still just two streets away from the coffee house where it all began and, in among the modernity, when a ship is declared permanently lost at sea it is still recorded in the Casualty Book with a quill pen just as it was 300 years ago.

CHAPTER FIVE

Gin Lane
TO
Gin Palace

117

Most of the drinking places introduced so far were created to fulfil a need, whether by travellers in want of accommodation, businessmen looking for a place to meet and transact business, or working men in need of a place to self-organise. These needs would eventually outgrow the drinking places that nurtured them and demand their own professional spaces. However, dram shops and gin palaces met a need that could never outgrow them; it could only fade or move on to new drinking places. The need met by dram shops and gin palaces was to get blind drunk in order to forget about the misery of life in Georgian London.

It is difficult now to imagine just how scary spirits must have been when they first rose to popularity. Now that we have heroin and cocaine available on our streets alcohol can seem tame by comparison, no matter how strong it is. But when spirits first emerged they were four times as strong as the strongest imported wine (available to the rich) and six times as strong as the strongest beer (available to poorer citizens). Spirits represented a big leap in the level of intoxication. To get very drunk on beer requires time and commitment, but with spirits it is more challenging to stop before reaching that point than it is to have too much.

Still, England lagged behind the Continent when it came to adopting

The GIN Shop.

"... now Oh dear, how shocking the thought is,   They do it on purpose folks lives to shorten
They makes the gin from aquafortis :   And tickets it up at two-pence a quartern. "

New Ballad.

Designed, Etched & Pub.d by Geo.e Cruikshank — November 1.st 1829.

spirits, as well as behind Ireland and Scotland, where whisky drinking quickly took deep root. The reasons why spirits did not take off in England were at first connected to availability. The main drinking establishments of the day, taverns and alehouses, could not sell spirits because they were still restricted to their traditional realm of wine and beer respectively. However, specialist houses had begun to develop by the seventeenth century. At first they were called a variety of names, including 'strong water houses', but by the mid-seventeenth century they were generally 'brandy shops' if they were of the better and the more expensive sort, 'dram shops' if they were cheaper.

The main limit on the popularity of spirits was the high price of the imported brandies, which were the most common choice. Very little whisky was imported from Scotland or Ireland until the nineteenth century, and at first very few English spirits were produced. The quality of the spirits that were produced in England was very bad. They were most often raw-grain spirits, made from unmalted grain, and were also usually made from spoiled or damaged grain. The only way to make them palatable was to flavour them strongly, and they were sold in a range of flavours such as aniseed or peppermint – but no particular flavour gained dominance or enjoyed much popularity.

Irish Whiskey.

Och! Judy dear, a fig for beer,
The pleasure sure is greater,
When you are dry, to bring your eye,
With quarterns of the cratur!'"

PREVIOUS | The skeleton of death lurks in the background of a cartoon warning that 'Some find Death by Sword and Bullet; And some by fluids down the Gullet', 1815. | OPPOSITE | Grotesque imagery of death is everywhere in this cautionary cartoon on the dangers of gin, 1829. | ABOVE | A short poem on the joys of 'the cratur' or whisk(e)y, 1831. | OVERLEAF LEFT | A short poem on English gin, 1831. | OVERLEAF RIGHT | A short poem on French brandy, 1831.

While they might have got into spirits around 150 years later than the rest of Europe, the English soon made up for their years of abstinence. A perfect storm of circumstances eventually came together in the early eighteenth century, which brought one particular flavour to popularity – and then through popularity into infamy. That flavour was juniper, and the spirits flavoured with it are better known as gin. England would eventually be consuming ten litres of gin for every man, woman and child every year.

In 1689 William of Orange took to the throne and adopted the favourite pastime of English kings: war with France. To fund

English Gin.

If trouble should chance to assail you,

& Fortune in malice should grin,

The cordial that never will fail you,

Is Seagers & Evans's Gin.

French Brandy.

Ah, ha, Mr Englishman! voyez ici,

De grandest specific to banish ennui,

Begar is a bumper of French eau de vie;

So here's the Roast Beef of Old England,

Washed down by the pure Coniac.

ABOVE | A novelty Dutch *genever* jug, c. 1750.

OPPOSITE TOP | Nineteenth-century botanical illustration of juniper. | OPPOSITE BOTTOM A travelling Dutch merchant selling *genever*.

OVERLEAF | A Man holds up a coin to buy a glass of gin. The distillery (possibly an illegal still) appears in the background.

the war while also hitting French trade with England he raised the import tax on brandy to eye-wateringly high levels, cutting off the supply for all but the richest. At the same time he decided to promote a home-grown alternative. In the early years of his reign there had been a glut of grain production, and landowners were having trouble with supply exceeding demand, causing prices to drop. A new market was needed, and increased production of spirits would be just the thing to take the grain off their hands.

To appease both the grain-glutted landowners and any spirit drinkers who had been priced out by the increased tax on brandy, William dropped the tax on native spirits to nearly nothing. As well as dropping the tax he deregulated their production and sale. In London this was a huge step, not only because the sale of alcohol had previously been restricted to a limited number of licensed premises, but also because almost every reasonably profitable profession was already heavily regulated by guilds and local ordinances. Becoming a baker meant undergoing a

seven-year apprenticeship, if you could find a master who would take you, but becoming a spirit rectifier and seller could now be done overnight without the need to ask permission from anyone.

Meanwhile the new Dutch court, and also the Dutch soldiers and sailors who accompanied them, had brought with them a taste for a new spirit flavouring. Dutch *geneva* was made by redistilling a heavy malt spirit with juniper berries and other spices. While the malt base did not take off, the combination of botanicals and the technique of flavouring by redistilling (or rectifying) turned out to be a very good way to hide the worst qualities of England's poor grain spirits and produce a drinkable product. The Dutch technique when applied to the English base spirit produced a whole new kind of spirit: gin.

With next to no tax to pay and the base spirit made from cheap excess grain, this new gin could be sold extremely cheaply. The price of the new spirits as well as their improved flavour won over not only some of those who had been priced out of brandy drinking by the tax increase, but gave a new taste for spirits to many who had never been able to afford them before. Dram shops and gin palaces proliferated,

DISTILLATIO.

In igne succus omnium, arte, corporum   Vigens fit vnda, limpida et potissima.

and nowhere did they find a more welcoming embrace than in the fast-growing city of London.

Between 1650 and 1750 the population of London doubled: an increase that was not held back even by the loss of more than a fifth of the population to the Great Plague in 1665, nor by the loss of large numbers of the city's buildings to the Great Fire of London in 1666. People were attracted from the countryside to the city by the rapid increases in trade, employment and wages. However, they also arrived in a city with no sewerage system, no public transport and only the most rudimentary provision of clean water. The housing available to new arrivals was both poorly built and in short supply, leading many to share cramped quarters.

Despite the overcrowding at home many workers did in fact have an increased disposable income and spending power. However, they had little to spend it on. Affordable consumer goods were limited, and the average manual worker was not welcome in many of London's entertainment venues. Even many alehouses had started to become picky about their customers, but the new dram shops would welcome anyone – or at least, sell to anyone.

There often was not much of a welcome to be had, with drams sold in cramped back rooms, from carts and over counters in grocers' and chandlers' shops. Dram shopkeepers in general could not afford for the room to be a social space. They were suppliers rather than venues, and most customers would be encouraged to come in, drink up quickly while standing, and then head back out again. Customers would return to work, go out into the streets or just keep walking along until they found another dram shop where they could repeat the process. But while they couldn't stay in the shop to warm themselves, the strong drink made walking the streets more entertaining and perhaps made them feel warmer inside.

One market woman testifying at a quarter session gave a fair account of what it was like to be a working woman in London in the early eighteenth century: 'My name is Mary Lee and tho I say it there is never a woman in the parish that takes more care for an honest livelihood than myself. I turn my hand to any thing to get a penny: Sometimes I sell things in Leadenhall Market and sometimes I do an odd chore at one house and sometimes at another. We Market Women are up early and late and work hard for what we have. We stand all weathers and go through thick and thin. It is well known, that I was never the woman that spared my carcass and if I spend three farthings now and then, it is nothing but what is my own. I get it honestly and I do not care who knows it; for if it was not for something to cheer the spirits, between whiles, and keep out the wet and cold; alackaday, it would never do. We should never be able to hold it. We should never go thro-stitch with it, so as to keep body and soul together.'

However, the new gin craze among the poor did not meet with sympathy and understanding from the ruling classes, nor from the middle classes, who found themselves reading scandalous stories in the new and rapidly expanding popular press. Working women in drinking establishments were especially demonised, as women had never been welcome customers in the inns, taverns and alehouses of the old order, and heavy-drinking women were viewed as even more scandalous then than some people find binge-drinking women today. An anti-gin movement was formed, aiming to save the poor from their own weakness by banning the evil substance. Pressure was put on Parliament, but initially the cause made little progress. One of the key turning points in their crusade against gin was the publication of the story of Judith Defour in 1734, which established forever the caricature of the careless mother, made neglectful or cruel by gin, later enshrined in William Hogarth's 1751 print, 'Gin Lane.'

The trial of Judith Defour in 1734 was widely reported in the newspapers, and it also attracted great crowds of spectators to the public gallery. Dramatically enough, Defour was on trial for the murder of her own daughter, and the story of the gin-soaked events leading up to the death was pieced together largely from her own testimony. Defour worked as a throwster, preparing silk for weaving, but did not earn enough from her work to support the young daughter who she was raising with only the help of her mother. A few weeks before the incident her daughter had been taken to the Bethnal Green workhouse because of Defour's inability to support her.

One Sunday, on her morning off, Defour decided to take her daughter out of the workhouse to spend the day with her. On her first visit she was turned away, but when she came back with a note of permission supposedly from the church wardens (which turned out to be forged), her daughter Mary was released into her care. In the evening Defour arrived at work as usual, and after a few hours she sent out for a dram of gin. It was not unusual to send out for a little gin while doing long hours of repetitive work, but not long after the first she sent out for

OPPOSITE | Early rectification of *genever* in alchemical-style glass vessels, late sixteenth century. from the Luttrell Psalter (1325–40). | OVERLEAF Three women distract a gin-seller's attention while a match boy steals her money, c. 1765.

What News? great News says Blab while Polly swills,
The raptur'd Landlady her Liquor spills, —

The GIN SH

Printed for Carington Bowles, Map & Printsell

...uls Church Yard, London

IS PLAYED.

The Match Boy artfully the Money steals,
The Basket Woman great surprize reveals.

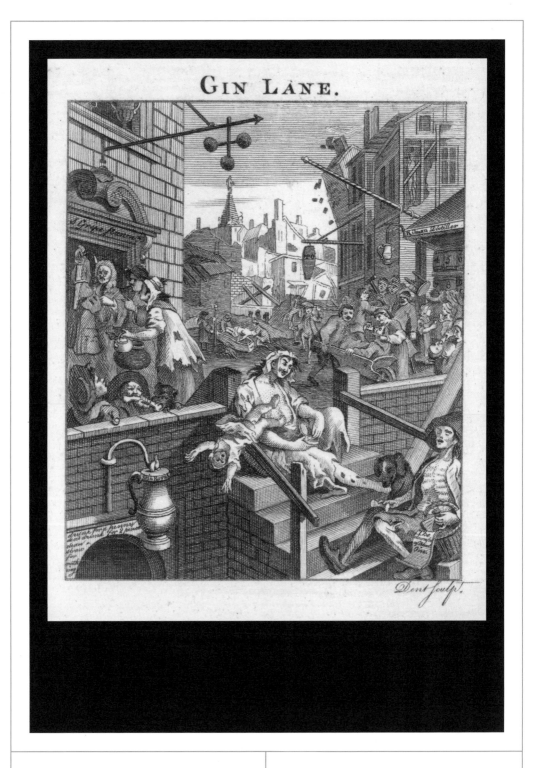

ABOVE | William Hogarth's 'Gin Lane.' | OVERLEAF
Satirical cartoon showing the 'Gin-Juggarnath'
crushing its worshippers beneath its barrel wheels.

another. A co-worker persuaded her it was a bad idea to have another gin so soon, and gave her a penny for a roll with cheese instead – but when Defour came back it was with a plain roll and another gin. After drinking it she broke down in tears and told a friend that she was racked with guilt because she had left her daughter lying in a field all night. She led her co-workers out to where she had left her daughter and they found her lying naked and dead of strangulation.

At the trial Defour blamed a vagrant, Sukey, but the woman was never found. The two women had only met that day and had been drinking together in the afternoon in the company of the child, until they ran out of money. Sukey persuaded Defour that they should sell the brand-new clothes the workhouse had given to Mary for money to use to carry on drinking. They took her out into the field and stripped her of the valuable clothes. Then, when she would not stop crying, they tied a linen rag around her neck with the intention just to quiet her but ended up accidentally killing her. Her mother testified that Defour had never been in her right mind, even before drinking, but she was sentenced to death anyway, and hanged.

The stories presented cast gin in the role of a villain leading the poor astray. With such an obvious villain available to blame for the desperate conditions, the concerned middle and upper classes could continue to ignore deeper social issues, such as single mothers unable to earn enough to feed their children, and concentrate on banning gin. The great gin ban was actually several laws enacted between 1729 and 1743, almost all as ill-conceived in concept and wording as each other. In the House of Lords the Earl of Chesterfield eventually said of the ban that 'If the promoter of the bill against gin had not been known to be a very sober man, I should have supposed him to be an excessive gin drinker.'

The most notable feature of the final ban was that it concentrated only on the sale of quantities less than five gallons, allowing wholesalers to continue to sell legally to retailers – and anyone with a decently sized cellar could continue to buy gin entirely unimpeded. As a result, from the first legislative attempt at a ban to the final repeal of the last law stretched a period of fourteen years during which gin was, to some extent, illegal to sell to anyone but the rich. The popularity of gin never wavered during that time and neither did its availability, although the quality certainly suffered. If anything, the illicit nature of the drink only made it more popular at a time when the Parliament that had banned it was extremely unpopular.

The ban was eventually lifted in 1743, and during the repeal debate the Earl of Islay made a speech that is now famous: 'The law which is hereby to be repealed was passed in a sort of mad fit, and has been an affront to our government ever since it passed. Every man who could foresee any thing, foresaw, that it was such a law as could never be executed. But as the poor had run gin-mad, the rich had run anti-gin-mad and in this fit of madness no one would give ear to reason.'

The repeal brought gin back to legality, but not respectability. Its popularity, in any case, was already on the wane from the dizzy heights of the craze, when one in every four buildings in London sold gin and the birth rate in London actually dropped below the death rate. It had been an unsustainable boom, and competition from porter – a new, stronger beer – was proving significant, at least among the portion of the population who were welcome in the alehouses. The new pleasure gardens, more of which had begun to open from

The GIN-JUGGARNATH. Or,

— It's Devotees destroy themselves — It's progress is ma

Designed Etched & Published by George Cruikshank. 23 Myddelton Terrace Pentonville March 1st 1835

orship of the GREAT SPIRIT of the age !!
ith desolation. Misery. and Crime ___

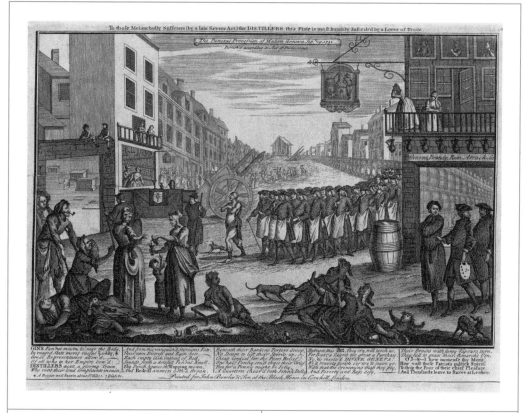

the 1730s, also provided entertainment and a space for socialising (including some notorious socialising between the sexes in the bushes), from just one penny. They provided a much-needed alternative entertainment to simply getting blind drunk on gin, although most were not exactly sober spaces themselves.

While the dram shops might have been reduced in numbers from the peak of their popularity, they certainly were not going away. They still remained, for one thing, the only type of drinking establishment that openly welcomed women. However, the lingering association of the dram shops with 'evil' women like Judith Defour meant they would never become a reputable place for women to socialise and organise themselves to become more significant in wider society. At least they provided an outlet for the frustrations of life in a society where women were legally the property of their fathers or their husbands.

Gin was still sufficiently popular at the beginning of the next century for a few enterprising publicans to find it worthwhile to clean up its image. Improved manufacturing techniques had lowered the price of plate glass, gas lighting and fine furnishings far enough that it was just about affordable to fit out a pub in fine style, even if it was a significant investment. Old run-down pubs were bought up and decked out grandly to become the brand new gin palaces. The first reported gin palace was Thompson and Fearon's on Holborn Hill, designed by John B.

ABOVE | Funeral for Madam Geneva on the day of the gin ban. | OPPOSITE | Etching of a gin palace, showing the patrons all drinking on their feet because of the lack of seating.

Papworth, one of the premier architects of his day. The style of its wide-open room with large windows and a long, polished counter was widely imitated, as were the bright gas lamps lining the front of the building, making it a beacon of light in the dark nights before street lighting.

There was, however, still one important feature missing from the typical gin palace. Despite the size and the grandeur of the palaces, there was no seating. The surroundings might have been better -looking but the customers were still encouraged to buy, drink up and go without hanging around and taking up space in between drinks. The more popular palaces managed an impressive turnover, some serving more than 5,000 customers every single day. While gin had become gaudier it had not succeeded in become more respectable, and the new palaces still came in for a lashing from the press, as well as

from emerging professional moralists. Charles Dickens himself painted a miserable picture of the gin palaces in his first published book in 1836, *Sketches by Boz*.

The attractive splendour of the gin palaces, open to all, would only be rivalled by the development of the music hall. In the music halls customers were encouraged to stay among the gilt and the gas lights all evening, and would even be entertained while they drank. As for gin itself, it would have to wait for the cocktail age to finally achieve respectability. By the time gin did find its clean new image there were, anyway, much worse intoxicants available than spirits – and alcohol was recognised

OVERLEAF LEFT | Habitual dram drinker drinks his at the bar. | OVERLEAF RIGHT | George Cruikshank's mid-nineteenth-century illustration of a gin palace, with patrons young and old.

THE DRAM-DRINKER.—DRAWN BY KENNY MEADOWS.

CHARACTERS ABOUT TOWN.

DRAWN BY KENNY MEADOWS.

George Cruikshank fect

The Gin Palace.

No. 1.

THIS is the *Gin-shop* all glittering and gay.

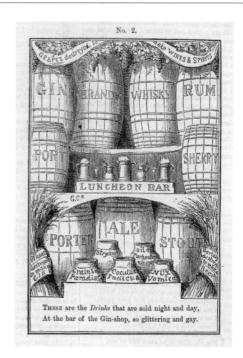

No. 2.

THESE are the *Drinks* that are sold night and day,
At the bar of the Gin-shop, so glittering and gay.

No. 3.

THESE are the *Customers*, youthful and old,
That drink the strong drinks which are sold night and day
At the bar of the Gin-shop, so glittering and gay.

No. 4.

THIS is the *Landlord* who coins his bright gold,
Out of the ruin of youthful and old,
Who drink the strong liquors he sells night and day,
At the bar of the Gin-shop, so glittering and gay.

ABOVE | An 'improving rhyme' about gin by George Cruikshank, 1868. | OVERLEAF | Two dandies take in a gin palace.

OPPOSITE ABOVE | London on a Sunday: a fight outside a gin shop. | OPPOSITE BELOW | Label for Coates Plymouth gin, 19th century.

as a rather milder vice by comparison. From the first import of opium from the Far East the concerned upper classes had a new spectre to blame for the state of the poor: drugs.

Yet despite the lessons of the past our drug policy has still not moved on today – the war on drugs closely resembles the 'anti-gin-madness' in everything except the target. We still blame drugs for ruining lives – and not ruined lives for causing drug dependency. We still think that a ban will eventually be effective if we can just keep tweaking the law to find the right kind of enforcement ... rather than considering the root causes of the problems of drug users.

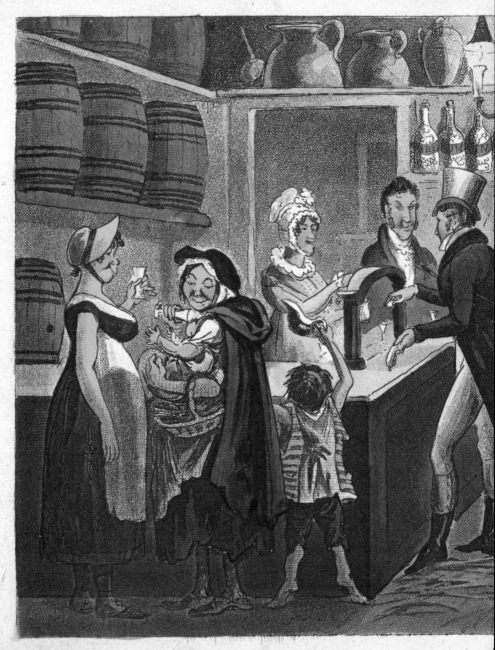

Tom & Jerry, taking B...

Pub.d by Sherwoo...

OLD TOM

Drawn & Engraved by I.R. & G. Cruikshank.

Ruin, after the Spell is broke up.

nes, Dec.ʳ 1, 1820.

CHAPTER SIX

TEA AND

SUFFRAGE

145

T ea first became fashionable in Britain after Catherine of Braganza brought a chest of tea with her as part of her dowry, when she sailed from Portugal for her marriage to Charles II in 1662. Tea had already been fashionable on the Continent for a number of years, the fashion having started in Holland and spread south. In France Louis XIV reportedly drank his daily brew from a teapot made of gold, and in Portugal it was also a habit at court.

The new queen brought the habit of drinking tea to the English court, and every fashionable person wanted to follow the trend she set. But the high price of the rare, imported tealeaves prevented the drink's popularity from spreading much beyond the court and the aristocracy. On top of the expense of the leaves, the disastrous way in which it was taxed when sold pre-brewed prevented tea from becoming a popular drink in the coffee houses. It was taxed by the liquid gallon, and any tea had to be inspected by excise officers between brewing and sale. They only came to the coffee house twice a day, so tea could only be made twice a day and had to be kept warm in-between times. It is perhaps not surprising that tea made up by

the barrel and kept reheated all day until it was stewed to death did not catch on as an alternative to freshly brewed coffee.

One reason for the high price was that the East India Company had a monopoly on the import of tea, and brought it in only in small amounts. Along with tea from China they also brought back from the colonial clubs of India the habit of drinking punch, made from a mix of spirits, citrus fruits and spices – including tea. As a consequence, in the late seventeenth century the most common way to see tea prepared in public was as an ingredient in a brandy or rum punch, where it could be served without the ridiculous by-the-gallon tax. Using tea for punch had the additional advantage of demonstrating your ability to afford the expensive ingredient – punch was a communal drink perfect for entertaining and showing off – while also reducing the amount of tea which was actually used by lengthening it with spirits and fruit.

At the start of the next century the quantity of tea imported by the East India Company began to increase and prices came down a little, stimulating demand. But although they had been somewhat reduced the prices were still kept high by the hefty tax applied to the tea (which was

now at least being sensibly taxed by the dry pound of leaf and not the liquid gallon of stewed, brewed tea). Throughout the eighteenth century smuggling in tea was extremely commonplace, and it was one of the most profitable smuggling cargoes alongside tobacco and brandy – but with the advantage of being much easier to handle than brandy by the barrel.

In the 1740s the cheapest grades of tea could be bought in Holland for six pence per pound and sold for four to six times as much, even when they were still being sold at half the price of legal, taxed tea. At that price and profit margin, smuggled tea was coming in by the boatload. It is estimated that at the peak of tea smuggling as much as four-fifths of all the tea in Britain was smuggled. In addition to the smuggled tea there was a more alarming market in counterfeit tea, made from everything from tealeaves that had already been used and dried out again to hedgerow leaves and even horse dung. The ingredients were not the biggest problem (well, perhaps with the exception of the horse

dung); the main thing was that most of the tea imported in this period was green tea. Black tea, which is the most common type drunk today, was not widely produced in China and only became common after the British began producing it in India in the mid-nineteenth century. Therefore the substitute teas had to be made to look green, and to get the best colour the counterfeiters coloured their wares with poisonous copper compounds.

Hiding a smuggling rate so high from the authorities without getting caught at the point of sale was only possible because tea was not drunk at central locations

PREVIOUS | Afternoon tea in a Dutch engraving, early 18th century | OPPOSITE | Women of the Dutch aristocracy take tea in a salon at one of their houses. | ABOVE LEFT | A less wealthy woman also takes tea at her home in the Netherlands. | ABOVE RIGHT | A Parisienne enjoys a cup of tea from a fine china tea set, 1799. | OVERLEAF | A wealthy British family sit down to tea, accompanied by playing on the harpsichord, c. 1745.

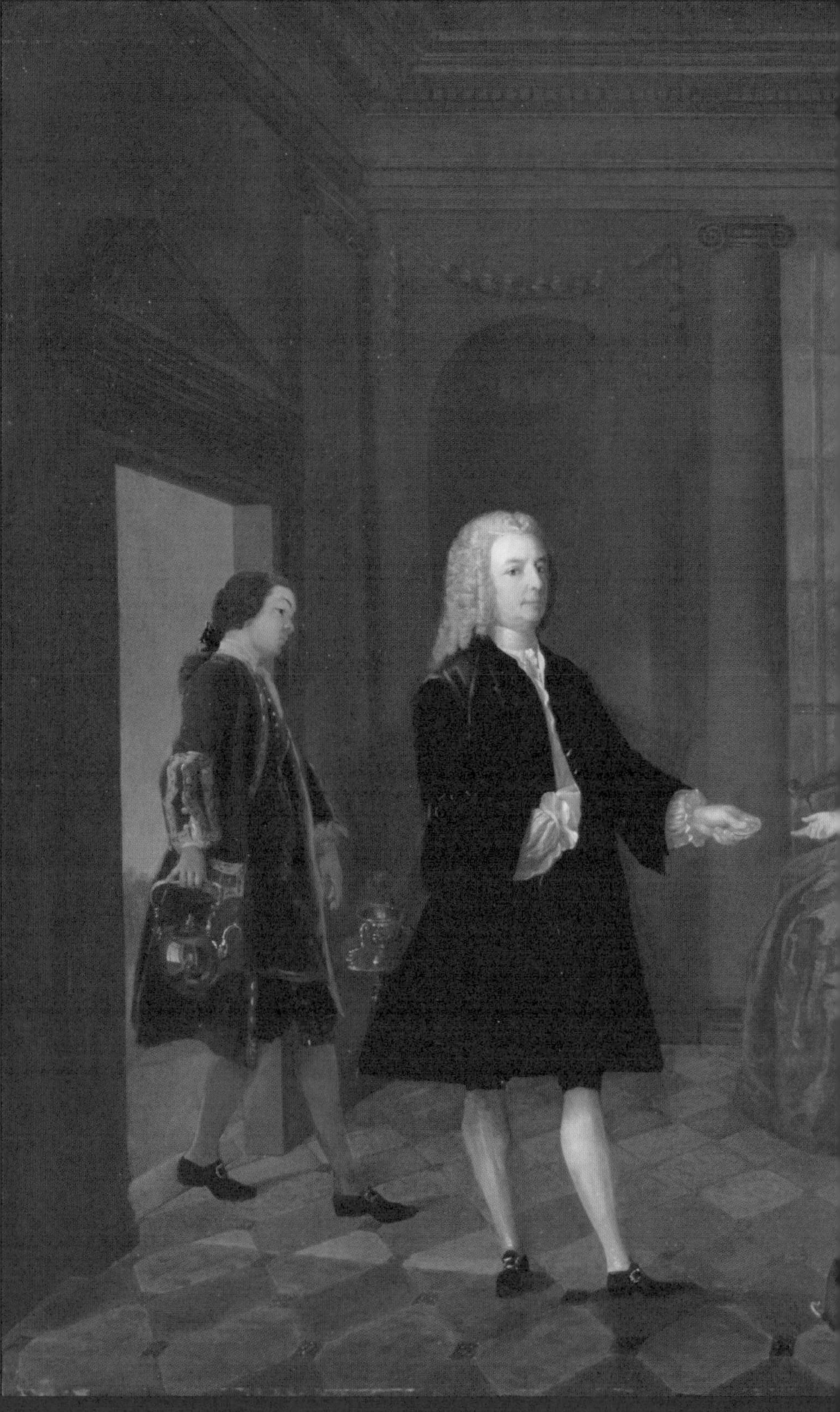

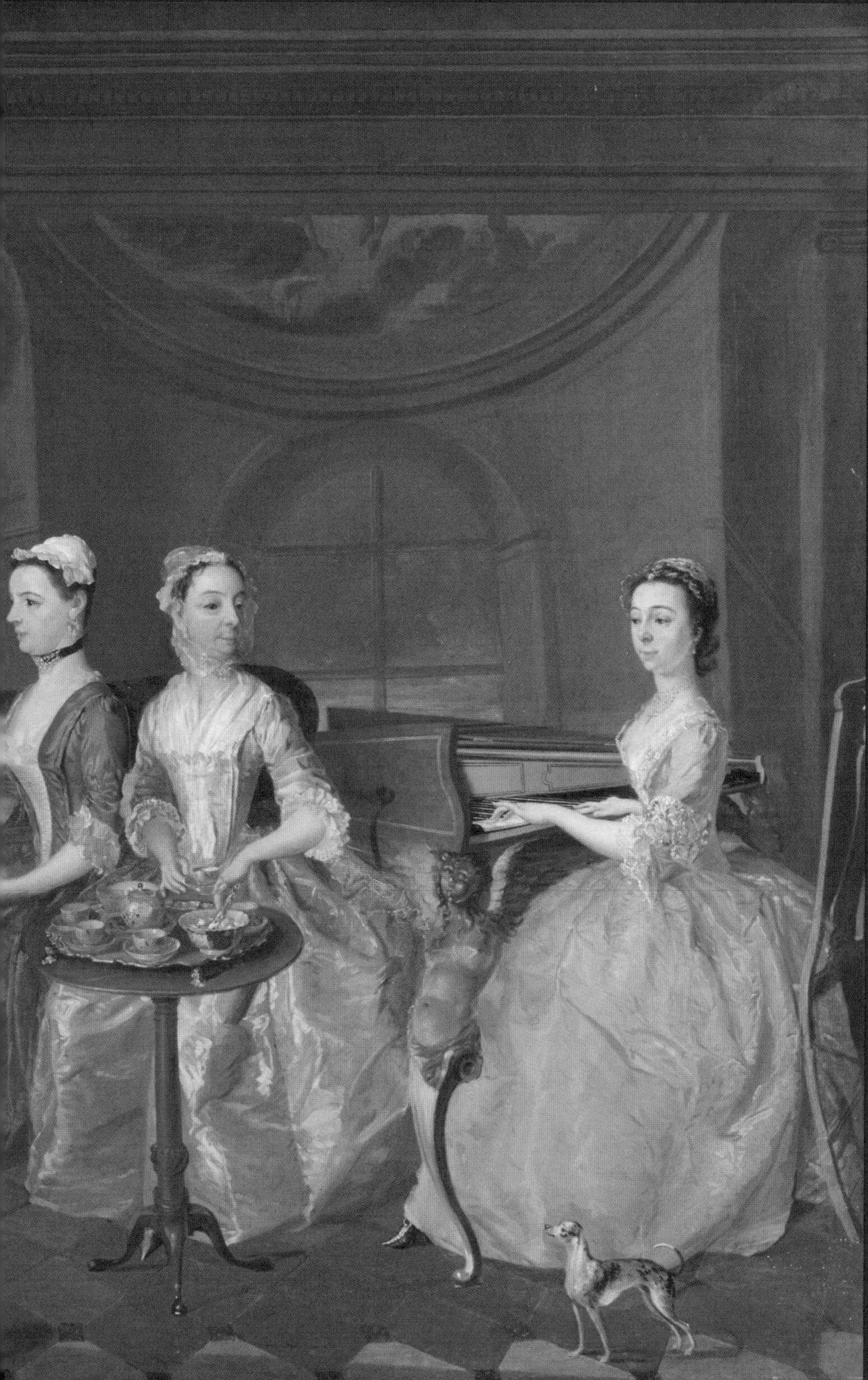

Ph. Mercier Pinx.t   Publish'd according to Act of Parliament Jan.y 1.st 1758   Rich.d Houston Fecit

Just risen from Repose fair Delia see;   Thus does the Nymph her Morning hours waste,
Sipping with secret Joy her favorite Tea;   And smiles indulgent on the glad Repast.

MORNING.

London, Printed for Rob.t Sayer opposite Fetter Lane Fleet Street. Price 1.s 6.d

ABOVE | A young lady takes tea alone in her bedroom to while away the morning hours, 1758.

OPPOSITE TOP | Tea plantation in Darjeeling, c. 1860. | OPPOSITE BOTTOM | Tea chest and tea caddies, c. 1790.

like coffee houses or taverns. It was most commonly drunk in the home, where the local smuggler or their distributor could make a discreet visit with a pound or two of leaves at a time. Smuggling died out when the tax was slashed in 1784 from 119% to just 12.5%, and consumption of taxed tea rose so quickly that within ten years the total amount of tax collected was more than it had been before the rate was reduced.

By the end of the eighteenth century the popularity of tea had spread throughout society, and it was recorded in the 1790s that a typical labourer and his family would use two ounces of tea a week, costing 5–10% of his salary when the sugar to accompany the tea was included. Annual consumption was in the region of £23 million, up from just £100,000 at the start of the century.

Although men and women both drank tea, it was primarily associated with women. Men had their inns, taverns, alehouses and coffee houses, where they drank in all-male companionship. Women were left with just the home and the tea table, always pouring and playing hostess. By the nineteenth century many women

had grown tired of this reduced role in public life and started seriously pushing for change.

Initially the focus was on access to education and on basic rights like the ability to own property, work for a wage or be granted a divorce. It is hard to imagine now just how reduced women's rights were at the dawn of the nineteenth century. In 1839 the Infant Children's Act gave mothers, for the first time, the legal right of access to their children, who had previously been wholly the property of their fathers. In 1849 the first further education establishment for women, Bedford College, was founded in London, although it would not be

The Daily Mirror

THE MORNING JOURNAL WITH THE SECOND LARGEST NET SALE.

No. 776. | Registered at the G. P. O. as a Newspaper. | FRIDAY, APRIL 27, 1906. | One Halfpenny.

SUFFRAGETTES WHO RIOTED IN THE COMMONS AND WERE EXPELLED.

The Ladies' Gallery at the House of Commons was the scene of a spirited disturbance on Wednesday night. When Mr. Evans was speaking on the motion for women's suffrage, shrill cries of "Divide!" and "Justice for women!" re-echoed through the House. A white banner, bearing the words "Votes for Women," was thrust through the grille. Finally the Ladies' Gallery was cleared by the police. Reading from left to right, the photograph shows Miss Kenney, Miss Billington, and Mrs. Roe. The two former took an active part in the demonstration in the House, and were forcibly ejected.—(Specially taken by the *Daily Mirror*.)

THE POOL FROM THE ROOF GARDEN OF THE LANGBOURNE CLUB FOR CITY WOMEN

On July 7, 1925, the Langbourne Club was formally opened, and there was at last provided a place where women who work in the City might lunch in peace and meet kindred spirits. The club is entered from Fishmonger Hall Street, a narrow lane leading out of Upper Thames Street just west of London Bridge. Next door is the great façade of Fishmongers' Hall. Members, of whom there are some 350, may treat their male friends to lunch, and there are organizations within the club which deal with dances, musical and dramatic societies, etc.

allowed to join the University of London for another fifty years. The Married Women's Property Act followed in 1870, giving women the right to own their own property for the first time.

But still, with the exclusion of private clubs and home salons, women continued to have few places where they could meet informally to discuss their newfound rights without risking their reputation. This untapped demand was waiting to be met by some enterprising entrepreneur … and yet the first new social space that welcomed women came about almost accidentally.

The Aerated Bread Company was founded in 1862 to produce a new 'hygien-ic' bread. Recent advances in the field of germ theory, which were not fully under-stood, had caused many people to distrust yeast. To capitalise on the desire for bread without yeast the ABC patented a new industrial process for producing bread by directly injecting dough with carbon dioxide – no yeast required. Although the technology behind the bread was new, the chain of retail bakeries that sold it was similar to any other chain of bakeries, until one London branch had the idea of offering tea and snacks to customers while they were waiting to be served.

The chance to sit and drink tea with company while taking a break from shopping proved so popular that in 1864 the ABC opened the first ever dedicated tea rooms in the courtyard of Fenchurch Street station. The ABCs took off and the chain expanded rapidly, opening many

PREVIOUS LEFT | Front page of the *Daily Mirror* after the expulsion of protesting suffragettes from the House of Commons, 27 April 1906. | PREVIOUS RIGHT | Women relax on the roof of the Langbourne Club, a private members' club for women working in the City of London, which opened in 1925. | ABOVE Ladies at tea in their home, 1868. | OPPOSITE A variety of traditional and modern china designs from Mrs Beeton. | OVERLEAF | Three young ladies enjoying tea in the garden.

new shops in London and elsewhere. They were self-service cafés, and at their peak of popularity in 1923 there were more than 250 ABC tea shops in London alone. The Lyons tea houses were founded in 1884, with a more upmarket model that provided table service – but to maintain their appeal to women the service was always by waitresses, never waiters. Tea shops also opened in all the new department stores that had begun to open up and down the country. The tea shop and the department store were a natural pairing, as both spaces were tailor-made for women to exercise their small newfound freedoms and to spend money that was finally their own.

The tea shops were the first acceptable places for young women to dine without a chaperone and to exchange ideas – often political ideas like the right for women to vote. Before the Reform Act in 1832 the idea of women voting had little

prominence among the many other reforms that were needed. Before that time the right to vote was tied exclusively to the ownership of property, and as that was a right still denied to women it would have been premature to start with a demand for the vote. However, the Act of 1832 and the subsequent Act of 1867 had opened up the franchise to a much wider section of the population, which included those without property and also, for the first time, specifically excluded women in the wording of the law. Small, local discussion groups began to form into suffrage societies, with the express purpose of pressing for votes for women, and in 1867 the first National Society for Women's Suffrage was formed.

That society was one of the precursors of the National Union of Women's Suffrage Societies (NUWSS), which would soon become the largest suffrage union in the country. The NUWSS organised rallies

A Packet for every Pocket

LYONS' TEA

Always the Best

and big meetings in public halls, but in between the big meetings the day-to-day talk of suffrage was still in the home, the workplace or the tea shop. By the beginning of the twentieth century there were, as well as the big chains, a wide array of smaller independent shops catering to specific groups. There were temperance tea shops, established with the specific aim of tempting men and women alike away from the pubs, and there were a number of specialist vegetarian tea shops.

The vegetarian tea shops were particularly known for being sympathetic to the cause of women's suffrage, and they were popular venues for meetings, dinners and fundraisers. Their popularity sometimes put them at the centre of the fight, as the scene of protest and direct action. It was in the Gardenia in London and the Vegitaria in Edinburgh that two groups of suffragettes concealed themselves overnight on 2 April 1911 as part of a mass campaign to

avoid the census.

The campaign slogans included 'If we don't count we will not be counted', and suffragettes hid themselves for the night in empty houses, in vehicles, on commons and in all manner of other places including a cave in South Wales. The group at the Gardenia were more comfortable than others, having repaired there for breakfast at 3.30am after spending the early part of the night concealed in the Aldwich Skating Rink. Although they evaded the official censor they didn't go entirely unnoticed, and police reports put their numbers at 200 women and 30 men.

The Gardenia was also used as the

OPPOSITE | ABC café in Ludgate Hill, London.
ABOVE LEFT | Early Lyons' Tea advertisement demonstrating the increased affordability of tea.
ABOVE RIGHT | Tea on the roof terrace of the recently opened Selfridges department store, 1910.

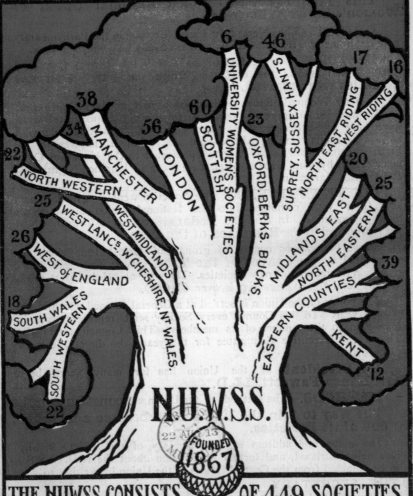

NATIONAL UNION
OF
WOMEN'S SUFFRAGE SOCIETIES.

6 46 17 16

UNIVERSITY WOMEN'S SOCIETIES

SUSSEX. HANTS

38
34
60
56
23
20
25

22

MANCHESTER

LONDON

SCOTTISH

OXFORD. BERKS. BUCKS.

SURREY. SUSSEX. HANTS

NORTH EAST RIDING

WEST RIDING

NORTH WESTERN

25

WEST MIDLANDS

MIDLANDS EAST

26

WEST LANCS. W. CHESHIRE. Nt WALES.

NORTH EASTERN

39

WEST of ENGLAND

18

SOUTH WALES

EASTERN COUNTIES

KENT

SOUTH WESTERN

22

12

N.U.W.S.S.

FOUNDED
1867

THE N.U.W.S.S. CONSISTS OF 449 SOCIETIES
UNITED INTO 16 FEDERATIONS
THE LONDON SOCIETY & UNIVERSITY WOMEN'S SOCIETIES.

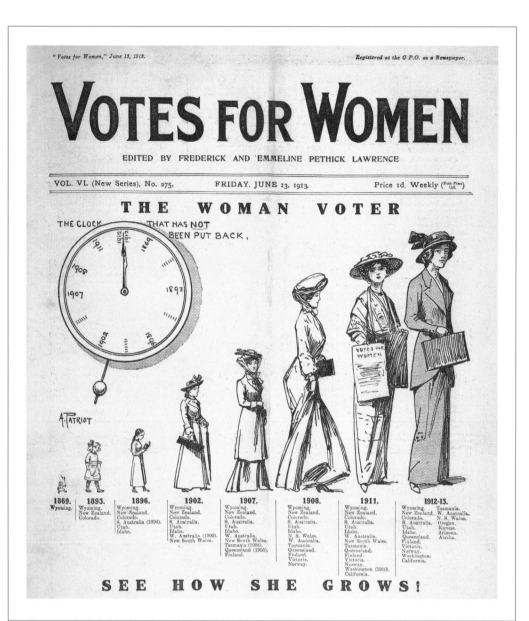

VOTES FOR WOMEN

EDITED BY FREDERICK AND EMMELINE PETHICK LAWRENCE

VOL. VI. (New Series), No. 275.   FRIDAY, JUNE 13, 1913.   Price 1d. Weekly (Post Free 1½d.)

THE WOMAN VOTER

THE CLOCK — THAT HAS NOT BEEN PUT BACK.

A. PATRIOT

1869.	1893.	1896.	1902.	1907.	1908.	1911.	1912-13.
Wyoming.	Wyoming. New Zealand. Colorado.	Wyoming. New Zealand. Colorado. S. Australia (1894). Utah. Idaho.	Wyoming. New Zealand. Colorado. S. Australia. Utah. Idaho. W. Australia (1900). New South Wales.	Wyoming. New Zealand. Colorado. S. Australia. Utah. Idaho. W. Australia. Tasmania. New South Wales. Tasmania (1904). Queensland (1905). Finland.	Wyoming. New Zealand. Colorado. S. Australia. Utah. Idaho. N. S. Wales. W. Australia. Tasmania. Queensland. Finland. Victoria. Norway.	Wyoming. New Zealand. Colorado. S. Australia. Utah. Idaho. W. Australia. New South Wales. Tasmania. Queensland. Finland. Victoria. Norway. Washington (1910). California.	Wyoming. New Zealand. Colorado. S. Australia. Utah. Idaho. Queensland. Finland. Victoria. Norway. Washington. California. Tasmania. W. Australia. N. S. Wales. Oregon. Kansas. Arizona. Alaska.

SEE HOW SHE GROWS!

staging point for a suffragette window-smashing campaign on 4 March 1912. Hundreds of London members of the Women's Social and Political Union (WSPU), the militant branch of the suffrage movement who had formed separately from the NUWSS in despair at its polite tactics, had made the first coordinated window-breaking protest three nights before with hammers concealed in muffs – and many had already been jailed.

Following their example, on 4 March members from as far afield as Scotland gathered to show their solidarity with the London branch and they went out once more to break the windows of the West End.

At the trial of one of these protestors the maid of the Gardenia gave testimony that rooms in the tea shop had been hired out to the WSPU. At the end of the night, after the arrests had been made, she went

PREVIOUS LEFT | Poster showing the spreading regional branches of the National Union of Women's Suffrage Societies. | PREVIOUS RIGHT TOP Three women (and their dog) show their support for votes for women with a picture of themselves at tea.

PREVIOUS RIGHT BOTTOM | Four suffragettes sit at tea in their protest sashes. | OPPOSITE | Front page of *Votes for Women* shows the progress of the movement worldwide. | ABOVE | Suffragettes break windows with hammers and stones thrown from slings as the police move in.

in to clean up the rooms and found a neat little pile of a dozen or so large stones still sitting in the grate. They were tied in brown paper and string, ready to be thrown, and one of them had 'votes for women' written on the protective wrapper, which was intended to prevent injury but also made a handy space for slogans. The café had been not just the meeting point for the evening of window breaking, but also the arming point where projectiles had been distributed among the participants. How the café staff had failed to notice the huge number of stones being brought in at the start of the night was a question left unanswered.

While the independent tea shops who were sympathetic to the cause had their windows spared from smashing, the chain tea shops were not so lucky. At least two branches of the ABC had their windows broken along with the Harrods and Harvey Nichols department stores. The anger of the café owners and shopkeepers, who felt they had done no harm to women and did not deserve to be the target of their protests, was addressed in a leaflet distributed by the WSPU:

> You, a prosperous shopkeeper, have had your windows broken and your business interfered with, you are very angry about it, and no wonder. But you are angry with the wrong people. You are angry with the women who broke your windows, whereas you ought really to be angry with the people who drove them to it ... 'Well,' you may say, 'I sympathise with the women but what have I got to do with it? Why should my windows be broken because Cabinet ministers are a band of rogues and tricksters? My dear Sir, you have got everything to do with it. You are a voter, and, therefore, the members of the Government are your servants, and if they do wrong, you really are responsible for it.

However, while the male owners of the ABC cafés certainly were voters, that was not true of all the independent café owners. A number of cafés did more than just cater for women: they were owned by them, and consequently they were more than just sympathetic to the cause, they were part of it. These tea shops would have been among the first businesses owned by women who had set them up independently, although for many years a few larger businesses had been run by women who inherited them from male relatives – as long as they could go without marrying, which would have given the business over to the husband.

Elizabeth Crawford, as recorded in her blog *Woman and Her Sphere*, has done much detective work to track these early female entrepreneurs from the scarce records that they left behind – records that were even more scarce than those of the average small business, when their owners were taking part in the mass boycott of the census. Following are some of the stories that she has revealed.

The Tea Cup Inn was opened around 1910 by Miss Marion Shallard and Mrs Alice Mary Hansell, the widow of a coal factor from Yorkshire. Mrs Hansell was the main force behind the business, and Miss Shallard left the business not long after it opened for reasons unrecorded. Mrs Hansell would have been 49 when the café opened, and she was a paid-up member of the WSPU, although not an active participant in the window smashing – or at least if she was, she was not caught and arrested.

The café itself was handily located just around the corner from the WSPU headquarters, a fact that she made sure to advertise in *Votes for Women*, the group's newspaper. She continued to advertise the Tea Cup Inn in the *Suffragette* after

the WSPU split in 1912, which shows that she took the side of the Pankhursts in the divide. Mrs Hansell continued to run her café throughout the First World War, and was still owner and proprietor right up until her death in 1923. She died a fully enfranchised voter, and when she died she had also improved upon the mere £87 left to her by her husband, to leave an estate worth £2,098.

Despite its masculine-sounding name, Alan's Tea Rooms was also owned and run by a woman. The owner was Miss Marguerite Alan Liddle, who opened the tea room in 1907, although she preferred to sign her name as M. Alan Liddle. The café was not as well located for radical circles as the Tea Cup Inn. Instead it could be found over on busy Oxford Street, tucked away up on the first floor of No. 263 above a dry cleaner, and accessed by climbing a narrow flight of stairs. Persuading weary shoppers to make the climb could have been difficult with a Lipton's refreshment

room on the ground floor just two doors away and a number of other cafés nearby. However, Liddle tempted them in with homemade lunches of several courses for as little as a shilling, and afternoon teas at a wide range of prices, again with cakes and sandwiches, which were all advertised as homemade.

As well as the public room there was a private room that was advertised in the *Idler* as being suitable for fashionable ladies to hold 'at homes'. At homes were popular with those who wanted to copy the upper-class habit of being available for visitors and entertaining at a particular time every week. For those who did not actually have enough space at home to entertain, a light and airy private room in a café was the best option.

ABOVE | The brutal force-feeding of a suffragette on hunger strike. | OVERLEAF | Female munitions workers at work during the First World War.

The room was advertised differently in *Votes for Women*, where it was stated that it was always available free of charge for suffrage meetings. Liddle's sympathy for the cause was in part a personal one as, although she was not a member herself, her sister Helen Gordon Liddle was an active member of the WSPU. Helen Gordon Liddle went to a number of WSPU actions, and she was eventually arrested for breaking the window of a post office after the group was excluded from a cabinet ministers' meeting in Manchester. She was sentenced to a month's imprisonment with hard labour in October 1909, and went on immediate hunger strike. While her sister served luncheons to fashionable ladies Helen was on hunger strike and suffering force feedings. She went on to write a memoir of her time in Strangeways, *The Prisoner*, which enjoyed some popularity when it was published in 1911. The short print run now makes the original a sought-after piece of suffragette writing.

The women's suffrage movement was at that time coming into full force, with the backing of a majority of MPs as well a membership in the millions, and it seemed about to succeed when the outbreak of the First World War caused campaigning to be broken off. A truce was called by the major suffrage organisations, and members threw themselves into the war effort. The cafés, meanwhile, stayed open and helped to keep the cities fed and watered through the crisis.

The war itself, and more particularly the labour shortage at home caused by the mass deployment, helped put more women into roles from which they had previously been excluded. Women took on jobs as ambulance and lorry drivers, engineers, munitions workers and every other traditional man's job on the home front. They served on the front lines as nurses and support workers, too, and many were killed.

When the war was over, the law had to be amended to prevent the disenfranchisement of front-line soldiers. They had been at war and out of the country for so long that they would no longer have met the residence requirement for the vote. The Representation of the People bill was the result, in 1918. After some debate it was decided to include the long-fought-for clause that would grant the right to vote to women. The clause passed through the House of Commons with a vote of 385 to just 55 against and through the House of Lords with 134 in favour and 71 against.

Within a year the first sitting female MP was sworn in – the American socialite Viscountess Nancy Astor. Despite being included in debates in the Commons she still found herself excluded from the bars and smoking rooms of Parliament, where habit proved more stubborn than law. The final assault on the male stronghold of the pub would have to be left to the next generation.

OPPOSITE | An illustration of Alan's Tea Rooms
from the *Idler*. | ABOVE | Women queuing up to
vote for the first time in 1918.

PICTURE CREDITS

All images © The British Library Board except

ACKNOWLEDGEMENTS

Thanks to my agent Lydia, without
whom I would not be a writer at all;
to all the staff at the British Library who
have worked tirelessly to make this into
a beautiful book; and to my friends who
put up with my sudden, over-enthusiastic
interest in the postal system.

THE BARMAID,

OR

SHE WAS A NICE LITTLE INNOCENT THING.

WRITTEN BY E. RODEN

COMPOSED BY F. W. VENTON

SUNG WITH THE GREATEST POSSIBLE SUCCESS BY

ALEC HURLEY.

Price 4/-

LONDON:

FRANCIS, DAY & HUNTER, (LATE FRANCIS, BROS & DAY BLENHEIM HOUSE) 195, OXFORD ST. W.
Publishers of
Smallwood's Pianoforte Tutor, The Easiest to Teach & to Learn from.
W. Stannard, Lith.